WHAT HAPPENED TO SIN?

The Truth about Catholic Morality

Charles E. Bouchard, O.P.

LIGUORI
PUBLICATIONS

One Liguori Drive
Liguori, MO 63057-9999
(314) 464-2500

*For Dad, Arlene,
Kay, and Maggie*

Imprimatur Potest:
James Shea, C.SS.R.
Provincial, St. Louis Province
The Redemptorists

Imprimatur:
+ Paul A. Zipfel, V.G.
Auxiliary Bishop, Archidiocese of St.Louis

ISBN 0-89243-849-5
Library of Congress Catalog Card Number: 95-80151

Copyright © 1996, Charles E. Bouchard, O.P.
Printed in the United States of America
First printing
3 5 7 9 8 6 4 2

Scriptural citations are taken from the *New Revised Standard Version* of the Bible, copyright © 1989 and from the *Revised Standard Version* of the Bible, copyright © 1946, 1952, 1971, by the Division of Christian Education of the National Council of the Churches of Christ in the USA. All rights reserved. Used with permission.

Excerpts from *The Gospel of Life*, copyright © 1995 by Libreria Editrice Vaticana, are used with permission.

Cover design by Chris Sharp

Contents

Part 3
Facing Today's Moral Dilemmas

Introduction

Why This Book? A Fresh Look at the Catholic Moral Tradition

The American writer H. L. Mencken once said that morality was "the theory that every human act must be either right or wrong, and that 99 percent of them are wrong." Oscar Wilde, in similarly cynical vein, said that morality is "simply the attitude we adopt towards people whom we personally dislike." Neither of these are very positive views of morality, but they represent how many people see it: as totally negative, or totally subjective and self-serving. When I tell people I teach moral theology, they often groan or roll their eyes, suggesting that morality is an unpleasant necessity, at best.

It's true that at its minimum, morality can tell us what we should not do. This book goes a step further. Its purpose is to paint a different picture of morality, one rooted in the Catholic tradition, which sees morality as a positive, creative capacity that helps us know not only what we should do, but what kinds of persons we want to be. It describes morality not as chafing under obligations of the law, but as a process of discovering happiness and real human fulfillment. This requires much more than a "no." The purpose of this book is to provide a brief summary of why morality is a profound "yes"—both to God and to human happiness—and of how the formulation of this "yes" is a lifelong project for Christians.

We sometimes think of morality as having mainly to do with obedience. That's part of the story. But morality is more than that. It is also a special kind of knowing, a "knowing what ought to be done." As such, it is different from knowing about something (for instance, theoretical knowledge about zebras or about the conditions that create snow); it is also different from productive knowledge, which enables us to produce or make things like chairs, airplanes, and apple pies. Moral knowledge is different because it doesn't merely tell us about something or about how to make something: it is concerned, instead, with human actions ("What ought I to do?") and character ("What kind of person do I want to be?").

This makes morality a very interesting kind of knowledge, one that draws on a whole variety of different kinds of wisdom, one that is at once extremely personal and thoroughly public, one that is both religious and secular. Discussions about moral matters can easily become emotional and even violent because unlike theoretical or productive knowledge, moral knowledge is something in which we all have a personal stake. It goes right to the heart of what it means to be human.

This book answers some of the most basic questions about morality. We will explore four basic areas: (1) how Christian morality developed; (2) how Christian morality differs from other ways of making moral decisions; (3) what makes Catholic morality different from other kinds of Christian morality; (4) how Catholic morality responds to important moral questions today.

Part 1, "Morality Becomes Christian," shows how Christian morality emerged gradually out of Jewish and Roman experience at the time of Christ. It suggests that because the Church is incarnated in various ages and cultures, the form of the Church's teaching of morality has undergone various "fashions." This is not to say that the basics have changed; rather, as Christianity itself evolved, the appearance of morality has moved from the relatively simple and uncomplicated moral life of early Christians, to the simple penitential discipline of the "Dark Ages," to the more elaborate approach of the medieval universities, to the highly legalistic and codified forms that were popular from the seventeenth century to our own day. Since 1965, Catholic morality has once again undergone a dramatic shift and is now in the process of constructing a new image for itself, one more suited to the thought and culture of the twenty-first century.

Part 2, "The Heart of Catholic Morality," describes several characteristics that distinguish Catholic morality from other forms of Christian moral teaching. These chapters touch on much of the material one would find in an introductory course in Christian morality. These introductory chapters do not in themselves answer specific moral questions but lay the groundwork and the method that will enable us to do so later.

We begin by showing how the way Catholics go about making moral decisions is one way among a number of others. We then look at the sources of moral wisdom, describing how Catholic morality uses three sources (human experience, reason, and Scripture) to arrive at conclusions about moral questions. Finally, we look at five major ideas—conscience, intrinsic evil, sin, virtue, and our liturgical and sacramental life—that give Catholic morality its particular "flavor."

Finally, in part 3, "Facing Today's Moral Dilemmas," we look at several areas that pose particular moral dilemmas for today's Catholics. We use the basic principles and theory developed in parts 1 and 2 to move toward answers for specific questions.

Throughout history, these questions have changed. At the turn of the century, for example, the morality of hypnosis was hotly debated. At other points in history, slavery, taking interest on a loan, and whether the newly discovered inhabitants of the New World had souls were the most pressing moral questions.

Today our complicated society presents dozens of such questions. We focus on four of the most important ones: sexual morality, healthcare choices and healthcare reform, the moral meaning of work, and the reconciliation of our political life with the demands of morality.

Throughout the book, I use the words *morality* and *ethics* interchangeably. The word *moral* is usually associated with religion or faith, but it need not be. Even nonreligious persons can have morals or live truly moral lives. Similarly, although *ethics* is usually used to describe secular "rules of conduct" (such as a corporate code of ethics), it can also mean a moral system based on religious faith.

When I use *moral theology,* I am referring to the systematic reflection on the moral life based on Scripture, revelation, and Church teaching. While the term *moral theology* is usually associated with Catholic morality, it is important to remember that any religious person who tries to bring his or her faith to bear on the questions "What ought I to do?" and "What kind of person do I want to be?" is in a broad sense a "moral theologian."

This is what makes morality such a controversial subject. Each of us has a keen personal interest in deciding what is right and what is wrong.

There are three pervasive principles that animate my understanding of the moral life. The first is that morality and spirituality are the same thing.[1] There has been a tendency to see "morality" as the basic obligations or laws that make us Christians, and to see "spirituality" as the collection of attitudes, prayers, pious practices, and devotions that help us grow closer to God. Throughout this book, when I speak of morality, I am talking not only about the norms, rules, and laws that help us shape our responses to moral dilemmas, but also about our overall orientation to God through prayer, liturgy, and acts of charity and justice. Because Christ was incarnated into human life, our spirituality cannot be reduced to spiritual things but must encompass the physical, psychological, and social dimensions of our lives as well.

The second principle upon which my understanding is based is that the virtues are truly the heart of the moral life. As chapter 7 explains, virtues are really personal qualities that enable us to become fully what God intends us to be. They are moral skills that shape our human capacities—desiring, knowing, fearing, and willing—and in so doing they enable us to blend our own natural gifts with God's grace. The violence and crime in our country are making it clear that laws alone are not sufficient to create order and peace in society. Peaceful countries are based upon virtuous citizens. Similarly, in the moral life, laws and rules are important guides, but true morality involves the development of moral character. Thus I invite readers to see the moral life not just as obedience to laws but as cultivation of gifts that draw us to God by making us better persons. This means that morality is not just for experts but is a challenge that each of us must accept. Wherever possible, I show how specific moral virtues provide the skills necessary for answering specific moral questions. In sexual morality, for example, the virtues of temperance and chastity are foremost. In business, fortitude, justice, and prudence play a primary role. And in medical ethics, justice is the animating virtue.

Finally, this book is based on the conviction that even though morality is intensely personal, because it involves my last, best judgment about what is good, it is not private. My hope is that the chapters on healthcare reform, sexual morality, work, and political life show that moral decisions on deeply personal matters have social implications, and political and economic questions must be answered out of the depths of our personal faith and convictions.

Because I believe that most good things are the result of shared effort and hope, I would like to thank all my students at Aquinas Institute of Theology. This book developed largely from my teaching efforts, and what I have written here reflects the wisdom, experience, and hard questions they shared with me. I would also like to thank Sister Diane Kennedy, Aquinas' Academic Dean, as well as the faculty and staff who have been so affirming of my modest efforts at education in morality. My prayer is that the Spirit will continue to bless our work so that together we might help reinvigorate the study of theology in the Church. Finally, I thank my moral theology teachers, especially Charles Curran, who instilled in me a great love for the Church's moral tradition.

Part 1

MORALITY BECOMES CHRISTIAN

Chapter 1

The Changing Shape
of Christian Morality

It seems like every day's newspaper carries another story of a problem in ethics: legal ethics surrounding a bribery or political scandal; medical ethics concerning organ donation, surrogate motherhood, or physician-assisted suicide; or business ethics respecting a corporation's violation of its public trust or the questionability of certain profits. We are sometimes left with the impression that ethics is a twentieth-century invention and that life in past times must have been simpler and less fraught with dangers.

In some ways that is surely true. Before highly advanced medicine, multinational corporations, or vast, televised election campaigns, life was simpler, and so were the ethical problems people faced. But every generation has confronted what it means to be moral, and each generation has had to work out specific answers anew. There are constants in our ethical tradition, but the detailed answers to specific questions require perceptive eyes and careful thought. While it might be true to say that ethical values are universal and unchanging, the norms that articulate them and reveal them to us change a great deal according to the society, times, and circumstances in which we live.

The Catholic tradition in morality is a strong and dynamic one. We can trace themes and principles that have remained constant almost from the beginning, but we can also see flexibility and accommodation as our moral understanding has responded to real changes in society and history.

The Emergence of Christian Morality:
The Patristic Period, A.D. 100–400

The earliest Christians lacked an identity of their own. Only gradually did they discover what it meant to be a church, or a community of those whose belief in Jesus made them different. Many early Christians expected Jesus to return sooner rather than later, and they did not see a highly developed moral system as important. Their morality was more a question of "living together until Jesus returned," so moral instruction was informal, pragmatic, and uncomplicated. Early Christianity was really a variation of Judaism, so early Christian morality resembled traditional Jewish morality more than anything else. As missionaries spread out and began converting non-Jewish Greeks and Romans, these converts brought their moral traditions (derived from classical philosophy) with them, and the emerging Christian tradition blended them in as well. This is precisely what was at issue when Peter baptized Cornelius, a Gentile, as related in chapter 10 of the Acts of the Apostles. After he did so, Peter's Jewish associates were shocked at his "immoral" association with a non-Jew. Peter had received a vision instructing him to eat meat traditionally forbidden to Jews, and God's voice had said, "What God has made clean, you must not call profane." Peter had realized that this meant that traditional Jewish law could be bent for the sake of bringing Gentiles into the Christian fold. As elsewhere recounted, Paul instructed Gentiles to refrain only from eating the meat of strangled animals, thus relaxing traditional Jewish requirements.

As Christianity continued to expand, it gradually developed its own ethic and its own moral structure. Even into the second and third centuries, however, Christian morality remained informal and relatively unorganized; early Christian thinkers might be said to have "made it up as they went along" since they faced moral questions as they arose and did not try to construct a systematic program of ethics. This approach was often exemplified in the treatises written on particular topics that were bothering earlier Christians. One such was "Whether the Rich May Be Saved," written by Clement of Alexandria in the second century. More and more Christian converts were prosperous, and the Church was trying to figure out how to reconcile their wealth with Jesus' exhortation to poverty, and specifically with the passage "It is easier for a camel to pass through the eye of a needle...." Many Christians felt that this made it impossible for wealthy people to be Christian. In a subtle interpretation of the scriptural witness, Clement said it is not what one owns so much as how one uses it, and that both the poor and wealthy alike must remember that they have responsibilities to one another: the rich to provide for the material needs of the poor, and the poor to preach the gospel to the rich.

The moral literature of the time was often rich in symbolism and allegory, which made it appealing and easy to remember. The Shepherd of Hermas, who wrote about the year 200, dealt with another specific problem arising from the fact that confession as we know it today did not yet exist, and people were often able to receive forgiveness only once, at baptism. What happens, he asked, to those who sin after baptism? Are they lost forever? Like Clement, the Shepherd dealt delicately with this problem but allowed one more reconciliation after baptism, which should not be taken lightly. He used colorful images of the Church as an old woman growing younger (regenerated by penance), the Church as a tower reaching to heaven, built of rocks (the faithful) taken from the stream (of baptism). These images stuck in the minds of listeners and helped them to absorb the emerging doctrine of sin and reconciliation.

Other early sources, like the first-century *Didache*, presented Christian morality as a choice between two "ways," the way of life and the way of death. Yet it allowed that there would be those people who could not accept "the Lord's yoke in its entirety," and they should "do what they could...." Much of the specific moral content of this document was simple common sense and was drawn from the prevailing secular ethics: shun evil, avoid anger, do not be fanatical, do not be a grumbler. Other ideas, like the prohibition of fortunetelling and augury, reflected the fascination with such things among early Christians.

After Paul himself, Augustine was probably the Church's first real moral theologian. But as was the case with most patristic moralists, his works, too, were occasioned by specific controversies and questions, not the least of which was his own struggle with sexual immorality and his own conversion. Yet his elaborate writings on sin, grace, and conversion became a rich source of moral teaching to which subsequent writers would return century after century.

Private Confession and the Penitentials: A.D. 400–1000

Unfortunately, Augustine wrote just at the close of the Church's earliest period of development. The fall of the Roman Empire, the Barbarian invasions from the north, and other cultural events pretty much "turned out the lights" on theological speculation and inquiry for several centuries. Although the years between 400 and 1100 are often referred to as the Dark Ages because there was little public intellectual or theological activity, the moral tradition of the Church continued to grow in monasteries and through the private moral direction monks provided to one another and to the laity who came to their doors.

This private moral counsel, which was the forerunner of modern day "confession," gave rise to a whole series of literature called the *penitentials*.[1] These were lists of penances to be assigned for various sins, and they give us a graphic picture of what daily life was like in this era, as well as how the Church once again adapted to changing cultural and historical circumstances. The penitentials speak of the usual sins like theft, lying, fornication, pride, and anger; but they also treat more exotic sins like bestiality, desecration of the consecrated host, incest, and pedophilia. In each case, the writers carefully distinguished the age, mental ability, and social status of the sinner and tried to provide an appropriate penance. Unlike the view held in recent times, however, penances were not seen as punishment for sin but rather as "healing medicine," which the priest (or lay monk, since these penances were not yet "sacramental" in our sense of the word and were often imposed by the laity) administered much as a physician would treat a sick patient. One writer, in words that are still good advice for confessors today, explained:

> Let the power of the physician become greater in the degree in which the fever of the sick man increases. Those who take care to heal the [spiritual] wounds of others are to observe carefully what is the age and sex of the sinner, what instruction he has received, what is his strength, how long he has remained in sinful delight....[2]

The penitentials marked a departure from the highly social and communal nature of moral discipline found in the early Church. We have already noted that for the first few generations of Church history, reconciliation was available only once; later, it became available somewhat more frequently but was usually public and communal in nature. Those who had sinned seriously, for example, were required to do "public penance," which might involve distinctive dress, banishment, or fasting, all of which would mark one as a sinner begging the community's forgiveness. These sinners would be reconciled as a group during the Easter vigil.

As the Church grew, however, and as early Christian idealism faded, communities began to realize that the Church could not be fully purged of sin until Jesus' triumphant return. The penitentials signaled a move from infrequent, rigorous, public reconciliation to private, personal confession—an acknowledgment of the fact that people sin repeatedly and that moral conversion is an ongoing process rather than a dramatic, once-and-for-all event. As a matter of convenience and to lessen the embarrassment of public penance, the priest came to stand in for the community as a whole, and he, rather than the community, became the agent of God's forgiving power.

The penitentials began in Irish monasteries but soon spread all over Europe as Irish monks went to Britain, France, Germany, and Spain as missionaries. Although some historians are skeptical about the origin of these books (one has said that many of the cases found there are surely "webs spun in the casuistry of the monkish brain...thought up in the cloister by the tortuous intellect of the clerical scribe"), there is no doubt in my mind that they are relatively accurate representations of the moral problems that plagued the Church in these ages, and that they describe a real effort on the Church's part to continue providing pastoral care even when cities, churches, and centers of learning had been debilitated.

In our own age, we have drawn a sharp line between "morality," which we often identify with law and obligation, and "spirituality," which we understand as having to do with prayer, the virtues, and our sacramental lives. Throughout both the patristic and penitential periods, however, no such distinction existed. Morality and spirituality—behavior and prayer, body and soul—were of a piece. So Paul, Clement of Alexandria, Augustine, and the writers of the penitentials would never have thought of placing morality in a separate category. For them, "morality" was simply the way in which Christians properly lived their lives, and this could not be separated from how they prayed or worshiped or "believed." In fact, it has been said that one of the reasons moral theology is so contentious is that "everyone is a moral theologian." This means that as soon as we make an act of faith in Jesus, we have to then begin to deliberate about how that faith affects the way we live. That is precisely what "morality" (or religious ethics) is. It is the search for a kind of behavior that is consistent with our faith.

The Systematic Development of Catholic Morality: 1200–1600

We have spoken of the Dark Ages as a period of cultural recovery, when intellectual and spiritual activity was quiet and largely hidden in the great monasteries of Europe. Although important advances were being made in pastoral care and moral theology, there were few means of communication, so very little information or thought was shared.

Like a sleeping bear awakening after a long hibernation, and for reasons not entirely understood, Europe awoke from its six-century cultural and intellectual sleep early in the thirteenth century. The so-called Middle Ages followed centuries of quiet agrarian life and were marked by the sudden and dramatic rise of great urban centers and an explosion of artistic and intellectual activity. Most of the great universities of Europe were founded in this period, and most of the great cathedrals—Chartres, Notre Dame, Salisbury—were begun.

As cities grew and flourished and more and more people moved from the quiet life of the farm to expanding urban centers, the Church realized that the quiet pastoral spirit of the penitentials, which had been the primary vehicle for moral instruction from the fifth through the tenth centuries, was no longer adequate. Urban life presented a whole array of new moral problems, not the least of which was the reappearance of dualistic and gnostic heresies like Albigensianism, which denied the goodness of created reality and established secret and exclusive societies that were at odds with Christian life. The medieval cathedrals, with their colorful windows and sculptures depicting the virtues and vices, the Ten Commandments, and important saints and feasts in the Church year, were a partial solution to the need for greater moral catechesis. The mendicant, or "begging," orders like the Dominicans and Franciscans were founded to provide preachers who could travel from town to town rather than staying put in their rural monasteries, and these orders were another way of meeting the need for education.

Faculties of theology developed, and theologians such as Thomas Aquinas, Bonaventure, and many others wrote great synthetic works of theology that tried to blend traditional Christian sources with new insights received from Aristotle and the other ancient Greek philosophers whose works were being rediscovered. These thinkers, who stressed the need to train people for life in the tightly knit cities of ancient Greece, provided the perfect basis for moral and political life in the rapidly developing cities of medieval Europe.

In morality, this resulted in a highly sophisticated picture of the human person shaped by moral virtues—skills that are acquired by practice and that begin to shape future behavior. Eventually, virtue shapes individual acts into inclinations to act in a certain way, and an identifiable moral character begins to emerge. We experience the fact of moral character intuitively every time we make a judgment about someone's reliability, truthfulness, or integrity. The fact that we can predict, to some extent, whether someone we know will tell the truth, finish the job, act charitably, cheat, or deceive indicates that we all have virtues—or vices—that shape our actions.

We speak of a virtuoso as someone who is unusually and naturally talented. Much like the skills of a talented violinist, the virtues of prudence, temperance, fortitude, and justice shape our moral ability and enable us to make good moral choices naturally and easily. Prudence, the keystone of all the virtues, is the ability to deliberate and choose well. Prudent persons are those who can naturally "do the right thing," those who seem to have an unusual ability to see reality as it is and consistently weigh the advantages and disadvantages of various choices to choose what is best in the long run.

Justice is the virtue governing the equitable allocation of goods and enables one to "give each his or her due." Temperance governs the human need for comfort and pleasure and enables us to seek the right amount—neither too much nor too little. The temperate person knows how much tasty food is reasonable, for example, and avoids both gluttony and excessive fasting. She avoids the vices of overindulgence and "insensibility"—the abnormal loss of all ability to enjoy pleasure.

Finally, fortitude is the virtue governing fear; it enables one to face obstacles to good choices courageously and overcome them. The mother who defends her children against danger and the judge who pronounces truly just decisions despite opposition, for example, both act out of fortitude.

Together, the virtues describe what it is like to be fully human, to fully realize human capacities for pleasure, courage, intelligence, and life in community. They are, as we often say, "their own reward" because just as the master violinist receives pleasure from playing the violin, so the virtuous person learns to "play" his personality to the fullest and to experience moral and spiritual harmony. The truly virtuous person is someone who has trained her various human abilities to work together so that—much as a finely engineered and well-tuned machine—there is a minimum of conflict and malfunction.

Sin is the deliberate choice of a lesser good, one that is less than fulfilling, not fully human. Vice, the opposite of virtue, is the acquired inclination toward sinful acts. Much as a poorly taught violinist consistently plays poorly, the "vicious," or vice-filled, person is one who deliberately chooses poorly again and again until the tendency to do so is deeply rooted and begins to influence future choices. Vice is a "bad habit"—not in the sense of an unconscious action like chewing one's fingernails, but in the sense of an inclination toward less-than-fulfilling, or sinful, choices.

The Legalization of Moral Theology: 1500–1965

Since there was no established seminary system at the time, the education of the clergy was unsystematic and often woefully inadequate. In the fifteenth century, for example, investigators discovered priests who did not know how many sacraments there were and who were using the "Hail Mary" in place of a prayer of absolution for confession. Although priests who aspired to university teaching (often members of religious orders such as the Dominicans and Franciscans) received a university education, most of the clergy engaged in pastoral care received their training through apprenticeship to older priests, and they were often not theologically prepared to answer the challenges of the heretical sects.

By the sixteenth century the problem had grown so great that the

Fathers of the Council of Trent inaugurated a comprehensive program of studies, based on the "short course" developed by the recently founded Society of Jesus, for seminarians who would deliver pastoral care rather than become university professors. This represented a vast improvement over the hodgepodge of education that priests had received prior to this time, but the short course was geared to pastoral care and was shaped by the growing practice of individual confession, which had not existed widely until this time. The Council Fathers were eager to assure a regularized confessional discipline so that priests everywhere understood the relative gravity of sin in the same way. Thus, after the sixteenth century, priests were trained primarily to determine two things: first, was there sin present in the penitent's confession? and second, if so, how serious was it? Although this approach had the admirable purpose of making the penitent's moral burden as light as possible by not requiring too much, it also shifted the primary understanding of what morality really was.

While through most of the Church's history morality was seen as the acquisition of virtue—skills for living rightly—the emphasis after the Council of Trent fell on avoiding sin. It was a subtle shift, but it had wide-reaching ramifications. Increasingly, morality became identified with sin, and the positive emphasis that virtue theory brought to the moral life faded from view. Instead of guiding people toward a realization of the fullness of human capacities, morality took on the features of a law book and asked only whether sin was present. Eventually, the virtuous life became almost solely the domain of priests and religious who had the time to pursue the virtues. The average layperson had to be content with merely avoiding sin and doing the minimum required by the law.

The moral literature of the period, the *manuals,* imitated the legal books of the time. They were highly codified and schematic and carefully distinguished kinds and levels of sin. Although geared to helping confessors accurately identify and absolve sins, they omitted the "heart" of the moral life and made morality look like a game of legal hide-and-seek. Many of the faithful lost sight of moral continuity and were unable to see morality as having anything to do with a good human life or with the cooperation of human ability with grace. They came to see it almost exclusively in terms of discrete acts and obedience to the law.

For a variety of reasons, this legalistic understanding of morality—

which made "moral" the equivalent of "legal"—became deeply entrenched and lasted well into the twentieth century. But it was a relatively late development and did not capture the fullness of the Catholic moral tradition. In time, the manual tradition, complex and detailed as it was, became brittle and unresponsive.

Vatican Council II recognized this and urged a renewal of moral theology; the manuals, which had been the sole textbooks of morality for more than three centuries, disappeared almost overnight. Although they had achieved an astonishing degree of conciseness and clarity, their main purpose, to help clergy determine the presence of sin, was inadequate for a changing Church.

The disappearance of the manuals, whose codified and legalistic method had become synonymous with moral theology over the centuries, created a huge vacuum in the study of morality. Although the Redemptorist moral theologian Bernard Häring tried to bridge the gap with his three-volume series *The Law of Christ* in the early 1960s, this proved inadequate, and he wrote another series, *Free and Faithful in Christ,* several years later. There were few textbooks, and many professors of moral theology resorted to their own notes or articles. Standardized textbooks began to reappear only in the early 1980s.

This period of transition created a great deal of confusion for Catholics who had learned to identify morality with legal obligation. They felt angry that the laws and rules with which they had been so familiar during their childhood were being abandoned or modified almost daily.

The problem was that most of these rules (for example, abstinence from meat on Friday) were never really a matter of morality but of Church discipline. They should never have been so tightly linked with morality. The importance that was given to these rules displaced and trivialized important moral matters like growth in good judgment and understanding of the values behind moral teachings.

Though it may have seemed that morality was going down the drain, all that was happening was a normal adjustment like many others that had been made in the course of Church history. Just as changing times required that the Church shift from the kind of informal morality that had characterized the early Church to the more detailed approach of the penitentials, so the twentieth century required a move away from the schematic approach of the manuals to one more cognizant of psychology and moral development.

Two important lessons are apparent from this overview of the development of Christian morality. First of all, as early Christian thinkers showed, we must not be afraid to find answers to new moral dilemmas as they arise. Just as Clement had realized that wealth posed a problem for early Christians who took Jesus' words seriously, so later thinkers have realized that nuclear war, interest on loans, slavery, medical technology, and AIDS pose problems that simply did not exist for previous generations and were not addressed in Scripture. The genius of the Catholic moral tradition is its ability to face new questions and search out answers to them.

Second, the history of moral theology reminds us that we must seek out moral wisdom wherever it is found. Since Scripture does not address every moral dilemma, we are sometimes left to look elsewhere, including to common sense, for answers. Because we believe that grace flows through human history, intelligence, and experience as well as through Scripture and revelation, we should not be afraid to look around us. This is precisely what Paul and the early Church leaders did as they gleaned moral wisdom from Greek philosophy, Jewish life, and secular literature. In a similar way, Thomas Aquinas drew on the prevailing philosophical wisdom of his day and appropriated the thought of the philosopher Aristotle. For us today, modern science, popular culture, history, literature, and the social sciences can all provide glimmers of wisdom and grace that we can confidently use to chart a moral course.

For Further Reading

Gallagher, James. *Time Past, Time Future: An Historical Study of Catholic Moral Theology.* Mahwah, N.J.: Paulist, 1990.

Häring, Bernard. *Free and Faithful in Christ.* 3 vols. New York: Crossroad, 1982.

Mahoney, John, S.J. *The Making of Moral Theology: A Study of the Roman Catholic Tradition.* New York: Oxford, 1987.

O'Connell, Timothy. *Principles for a Catholic Morality.* New York: Harper and Row, 1990.

Chapter 2

How Catholics Make Moral Decisions

Although the development of Christian morality has its own distinct history, it is part of a larger picture that includes many other ways of making moral decisions. Let us look at each of a number of possibilities and then locate the Catholic approach among them.

Morality As a Particular Kind of Knowing

When someone says, "Two plus two equals four," anyone who understands the terms knows the truth of the statement. This kind of knowledge is straightforward and doesn't admit of much dispute or argument. Moral knowledge—the kind involved in a statement like "you ought to do this"—is of another sort, however. Although it does have an objective dimension to it (that is, it is not merely opinion), it is much more flexible and often admits of argument or even controversy. In many cases, when someone says, "That is immoral," there are five other people who are willing to say, "That is not immoral" or "It depends." Even at its best, morality is an imprecise science because it deals with human behavior rather than with hard scientific facts or abstract theory.

Kinds of Moral Decision Making

The fact that human persons are made in the image of God means that they are blessed with intelligence and reason. This enables them to make moral decisions; that is, in many situations in which they find themselves, they must somehow decide what to do when faced with particular choices. We must decide whether to lie or tell the truth, whether to spend money or save it, whether to get married and to whom, and thousands of other things. Many of these decisions are simple and unimportant (for example, whether I buy a green car or a blue one), but others can have deep and far-reaching implications in our lives, such as the choice to marry, have children, or build a business on unfair or illegal practices. All of these decisions are "moral" because they are choices about values, that is, about what we want to preserve, what we ought to do, and who we want to be. When we fail to make moral decisions, we have given up our freedom and are allowing something or someone else to determine the course of our lives. None of us wants to do that.

Morality As Feeling

There are many different ways in which people make moral choices, however. Some people rely heavily on their feelings or intuitions to tell them what course of action they should follow. When faced with the possibility of taking property that rightfully belongs to another, for example, someone might experience emotional revulsion and say, "I just don't feel that it is the right thing to do." If pressed, they might say, "I don't know why, but it just doesn't feel right." In this case, a moral choice would arise primarily from an emotional reaction and would be like saying, "Theft really makes me angry." Similarly, we might rely on a kind of moral intuition, or little voice, that tells us what is right and wrong. Like so-called "feminine intuition," moral intuition "just knows" moral truth. That knowledge can be accurate and penetrating. But it also is hard to explain to others. Someone who makes moral decisions on the basis of an intuition may be absolutely convinced of the rightness or wrongness of the choice but cannot explain it to anyone else because intuitions and emotions are essentially private and individual. When we decide by saying, "I feel," we are in our own world of moral opinion. Authentic moral decision making, on the other hand, must be more than a private feeling and must involve discussion and dialogue with others.

Morality As Duty

There are other ways of making moral decisions, those based on rules against which we compare our behavior to determine its moral correctness. These approaches formulate rules by asking one of two questions: "What is my duty?" or "What will make me happy?"

The first approach to morality begins with the authority of a lawmaker and establishes our duty to obey. In this approach, the main virtue is obedience to the will of the lawmaker, at least as far as this can be determined, and this approach does not encourage discussion or questioning. It is similar to the parent who tells a child to do something. When the child asks, "But why?" many parents, knowing that explanations are usually not the beginning of better obedience, simply say, "Because I said so, that's why." In this case, the parent is placing a duty to obey upon the child. She is asserting her authority as the one who knows what is good for the child, and her rules require obedience. She knows that in many cases it is better to rely on authority than to get into a lengthy discussion of why she demands this particular course of action from the child.

Decision making based on duty can take many shapes. Some approaches have tried to use reason to arrive at moral norms that are absolute and universal and apply to everyone without exception. One such norm might be "Do nothing which you would not want everyone else to be able to do as well." On that basis, for example, we could rule out lying or theft, since none of us would want to be lied to or burglarized. Here the "authority" is reason itself, which has construed these absolute rules for human behavior.

Another kind of duty-based morality more familiar to us today is biblical, in which the authority is the word of God. Here the will of God is known to us through Scripture, and our duty is to obey it. This method is largely characteristic of some fundamentalist kinds of Christianity, in which moral truth is sought exclusively in Scripture and imposes an absolute duty to obey. Some people regard even the questioning of these scriptural norms as the beginning of disobedience. The problem, as we will discuss later, is that Scripture does not treat of every moral question we face today, and we have always made some scriptural norms (for example, the prohibition of killing) more binding than others (for example, turning the other cheek). This in itself is a process of interpretation that prioritizes the scriptural word and makes some passages more binding than others.

Morality As the Search for Happiness

Catholic morality is often caricatured as authoritarian ("Do what Father says"), but in fact it is not. Rather than making obedience and duty the primary components of morality, the heart of Catholic morality is in the notion of happiness, which is, as Augustine and Thomas Aquinas agreed, the purpose of human life, or the reason for which we exist. God created us to be happy and has planted this desire for happiness deep within us. So morality is not merely a matter of obedience to some external authority but rather the search for real, enduring satisfaction in life. For this reason, Catholic morality is goal-based rather than duty-based, and the goal God asks us to seek is happiness and human fulfillment. The Baltimore Catechism used to ask, "Why did God create me?" and we answered, "To know him, love him, serve him in this world and be happy forever with him in the next." That answer reminds us that God created all of us—even those who do not know God or believe in him—to be with him. When we are truly happy and fulfilled as human persons, we know that we have discovered some of that plan for us, and we have begun to discover what it means to be moral.

This plan is like the operating instructions that accompany a fine piece of equipment. To make the equipment function well, there are certain things one must do and certain other things one must not do. One should not, for example, put sand in a coffee maker: doing so would violate the "purpose" of the coffee maker and would probably ruin it. Similarly, the human person is a finely tuned, divinely created organism that has a purpose. Some kinds of behavior are "good for us," or make us happy and well-functioning, while other kinds of behavior are bad for us and impair our performance. The things that contribute to real well-being and long-term happiness are what we call morality. Those that violate us, make us miserable, and offend God's good wishes for us are immoral, or sinful. We say, for example, that when freely chosen, excessive drinking is morally wrong because humans fall far short of who they can be when they stagger, stammer, get sick, and suffer hangovers. Too much (or too little) of any thing unbalances us and makes us less than we should be.

So morality is not simply a process of obeying a set of written instructions with no idea as to why we should do so; rather, it is a process of discovering, over a lifetime, what is truly fulfilling and healthy for us. Parents must sometimes tell children to do something "because I said so." But for adults, morality becomes a process of discovering God's built-in plan for us, and we must learn what really fulfills and brings happiness in the long run. This last qualification is important because otherwise we end up absorbed in instant gratification, seeking pleasure only for the moment. Rather than saying, "I will steal this television because there is a program I wish to see this evening," we might say, "I wish to see this program today, and it is a good program that would make me a better person. But in the interest of justice and the security and trust of my neighbors, I will not steal a television to do so." In this process we have taken one good (the admittedly helpful television show) and subordinated it to another, more important good (justice and community security) and have thereby chosen the long-term good over the short-term one.

Catholic morality does not ask us to obey blindly but to understand why these teachings really lead us to fulfillment. This is obviously not child's play. It is an adult skill that is acquired only with some experience and help. I have met many adults who have never moved beyond a fourth-grade, authoritarian understanding of morality and who find the equation "morality equals happiness" threatening. They prefer the security of "being told what to do" rather than taking the time and energy to deliberate about what will truly bring them happiness and fulfillment in the long run. Moral education is of great concern to parents today. It may begin with "Do this because I said so," but it cannot stop there. At some point, children must be introduced to the notion of real, fulfilling human goods and be taught to discover those goods themselves. They must learn that "virtue is its own reward," that we seek morality not because someone tells us to but because we know it is a good thing.

In our system of morality, there is only one basic question, namely, "Will this choice make me truly happy?" Catholic morality starts with what is naturally fulfilling, but it does not stop there. When I teach morality, I often like to talk about "happiness with a small *h*" and

"Happiness with a big *H*." Happiness with a small *h* refers to those things that fulfill us as human persons—things like justice, temperance, truthfulness, community, fidelity, and so on. These are things all human persons—not just Catholics—need to survive and be happy.

These natural human values prepare us for Happiness—with a big *H*—which we sometimes describe as "heaven," or ultimate union with God. This means that when God calls us to be with him in heaven, he does so not *in spite of* what is good about human existence, but rather *by means of* the real human values we feel and touch and enjoy. This is what Thomas Aquinas meant when he said, "Grace perfects nature": when we are really "enjoying ourselves," in the sense that we have realized some of what it means to be truly and fully human, we are "on the track" toward heaven. When we are fully human—fully truthful, fully faithful, fully healthy, and fully just—when our human nature is all it can possibly be, we are open to grace. Grace enters in and completes God's creative act not by altering or changing the goodness of human values, but by perfecting them or "raising the voltage" on them, enabling us one day to actually see God face-to-face.

Speaking of Roman Catholicism, someone once remarked, "Wherever the Roman sun does shine, there's plenty of laughter and good red wine." Practically, this means that Catholics do not see holiness and happiness as incompatible. We don't feel that "anything that feels good must be a sin." Catholics are often uncomfortable about sudden, radical religious conversions that change personalities. Although such conversions do take place, they would be the exception, according to the Catholic understanding of grace: we believe that God prefers to "work through" us, gradually enhancing what is naturally good about us by grace, rather than radically destroying us and replacing us by grace. This is why the Church has repeatedly denounced heresies that deny the goodness of human nature. Human nature, far from being the "root of all evil," is good basic material that is not obliterated by grace but made better and perfected by it. Human enjoyment is not grace's enemy, but its foundation.

Chapter 3

Sources of Moral Wisdom: Experience, Reason, and Scripture

We have shown how Catholic morality, at its root, is a search for happiness and human fulfillment. But how do we go about finding it? Our tradition offers us three rich sources: human experience, reason, and Scripture.

Finding Happiness through Experience and Reason

I was once explaining to my mother, who is not Catholic, what a moral theologian does for a living. I told her I try to teach people how to think about moral issues, use the Bible in morality, and arrive at good moral decisions in medical ethics, sexual morality, and public policy. "Goodness," she said, "I don't know how you would teach people all those things. You just know what to do and then do it."

My mother's response is an accurate picture of Protestant ethics, which tends to rely heavily on the Bible and on one's personal reflection on God's will in our lives. Catholic morality, on the other hand, is systematic, often looks like a lawbook, and is not always directly derived from Scripture. It has a long and sometimes mysterious history and can be baffling to those who do not understand its roots.

The term *moral* means simply "what we ought to do," and we make moral decisions in many different ways. Sometimes we rely on our emotions or on a "sixth sense" to "feel" the right course of action. Other times, like many in the Protestant tradition, we look to the Bible for moral answers. Still other times we avoid religion or theology altogether, preferring to use reasoned reflection about human experience to come to sound ethical conclusions. The Catholic moral tradition uses all three—emotions, the Word of God, and reason—to shape its approach to moral decision making. But if one thing characterizes the Catholic approach, it is our reliance on reason and common sense to arrive at "what we ought to do" and our belief that any person of goodwill, even a non-Christian, can live a morally good life by carefully reflecting on moral choices.

The reason for this lies in the Catholic belief that grace (that is, God's creative power) is present in our very natures. Even though Catholics are sometimes seen as being obsessed with sin, our theological tradition is a very optimistic one. We do not believe that the human person is depraved, perverse, or naturally sinful. Rather, we believe that God created us good and that we participate in God's own life. This makes us essentially good, though certainly our freedom and the reality of original sin make the struggle for holiness a difficult one.

So while Catholics have at times found a certain fascination with "sins," in the last analysis we believe that grace has already made us good, and we do not get bogged down in the notion of "sin" as a condition that totally corrupts the human person. This belief is at the root of our practice of frequent confession: it is not a way of emphasizing how sinful we are at our core but a way of describing that we are restored to our natural goodness when sins are healed by God's renewing grace.

This fundamental optimism about the person has important implications for the way in which we make moral decisions. If we truly thought human beings were depraved and fundamentally flawed by sin, we could not trust the human mind to work well enough to know moral goodness and make sound decisions. Such a view would lead us to depend entirely on the scriptural word of God rather than upon God's grace in our lives. It would also make the moral life a series of individual, disconnected choices but would not necessarily help us be "good persons" who would gradually develop virtues and moral skills. Catholics tend to favor the view that grace is present in us in such a way that to some extent we can "trust" our minds and hearts to know moral good and choose it. This means that we can, to some extent, trust our human experience to tell us what is morally good and bad. Through careful reflection, we can discover that those things we experience as pleasant, fulfilling, and wholesome are "good," and those things that are painful, limiting, and frustrating are "bad."

Thomas Aquinas wrote that human persons are not created just in the image of God, as static images in a mirror, but "*into* the image of God," in the sense of a dynamic movement toward fuller union with God. This means that by grace we grow to be more and more like God, actually knowing some of God's plan for us. And although some of this plan is revealed to us in Scripture, many of the details, especially in moral matters, are discoverable by reason or common sense—the one ability humans alone possess and which has always been understood as making us closest to God. Our reason, though certainly able to make mistakes and choose selfishly, is a "spark of divinity" that can be trusted, with the help of grace, to see reality clearly enough to make good moral decisions. This is an astounding ability that gives us as humans a tremendous dignity and responsibility. In giving us the gift of reason, God has given us a truly graced freedom. We are not entirely reliant on external directions but have built-in "moral compasses" that, when properly trained, can help us discover holiness and true human happiness.

Natural Law: Knowing by Being

While Scripture obviously plays an important part in moral decision making, I would like to focus briefly on our rational moral decision-making ability, what theologians call natural law.

Natural law is frequently misunderstood and even abused, but it is the heart of the moral tradition in Catholicism. Let me highlight a few important facts about natural law and the role it plays in morality.

First of all, natural law is only "law" in a certain sense. In general, law can be described as "a reasonable rule enacted for the common good." Within that general definition, there are different levels of law. The eternal law, for example, is the plan for all creation that is in the mind of God, much like the plan for a new building is in the mind of an architect. Divine law articulates parts of that plan; the prescription to love one's neighbor would be a good example. Natural law is one step lower and contains those parts of God's plan that may not be found explicitly in Scripture but that are discovered through discussion, research, and dialogue. Natural law itself has levels, too, from the most general, like "do good and avoid evil," to more and more detailed rules that require more thought, such as "honor the elderly," "charge reasonable interest on loans," and "control the possession of dangerous weapons." These moral rules are all based on reason, but the more detailed they become, the more controversy they engender. Current disputes about gun-control laws certainly prove that.

Civil laws are those with which we are most familiar and include local, state, and federal laws enacted by legislatures. These laws, if they are good ones, clearly reflect the general definition above: they are rational, clearly known to the public they bind, and directed to the good of all rather than to merely private goods. This is why we see as undesirable those laws enacted simply to favor a particular politician's own narrow interests. These laws, while related to natural law because they are rational, are much more specific than natural law and much less flexible.

The second important fact about natural law is that it is based on human nature. (It is important to note that natural law is not the same as the laws of nature, which are animal instincts and physical laws that determine the boiling temperature of water and the amount of wing surface and thrust necessary to lift a jet safely off the ground.) Natural law is unique to humans because it is a process of rational thought (of which only humans are capable), which looks at human nature and tries to determine what is good for humans, that is, what is moral. In this sense, we "know by being": as we understand who we are, we are able to formulate some rules for what will make us truly happy.

"Nature," as it is understood here, is a complex and sometimes elusive reality. Discovering what "human nature" is requires the expertise of the biological and physical sciences, psychology, spirituality, and philosophy. Since the human person is mysterious, we never fully discover what it means to be a person, and our understanding is always evolving. This is why there is a historical dimension to human nature. Human persons are products of culture and history, and when asking, "What is human nature," we must also ask, "How have the forces of history and culture shaped human nature?" Are twentieth-century Americans, for example, essentially the same as people living in China in 5000 B.C.? There are certainly some things that remain constant about human nature, but changes and developments occur as well, so we must be careful to understand what we mean by "person" to determine what kinds of behavior best fulfill that person.

Nature also has a social dimension to it since human beings do not exist in the abstract but only in community. So when we ask what is "natural," we must take account of the community in which we live. Morality cannot be a question only of what is good for me, as a solitary individual, but it must consider what is good for me as a member of society. My good and my moral choices are linked to the good of those around me. This social dimension of natural law reminds us that it touches all areas of morality and not just biology or sex, with which it is commonly linked.

One of the most important things about our natural-law tradition is that it enables us to talk about ethical matters with people who do not share our religious beliefs. This is why the American bishops, for example, were able to write pastoral letters on nuclear war and the economy that received considerable interest from the rest of society. The White House, in fact, wrote a letter to the bishops as they were formulating their pastoral letter on nuclear arms, questioning their teaching on the deterrent value of nuclear weapons. The statements made in the bishops' letters were not based solely on Scripture (which would have rendered them largely irrelevant to nonbelievers) but on rational arguments rooted in common human values that other members of a pluralistic society—including White House policymakers—could understand and debate. The just-war theory, which tries to limit both the justification and extent of warfare, was developed largely by Roman Catholic theologians. It has been an important part of political theory for centuries because it was written in natural-law terms that make it understandable to nations all over the world.

Catholicism's natural-law tradition puts the Church in a unique position in society. While we can speak confidently about morality from a religious perspective, we are also able to speak about it in human terms that are understandable to others who do not share our religious beliefs. What is more, we can do so knowing that when we discover something that is truly fulfilling on a human level, we have at least the foundation for grace and supernatural fulfillment. We are thus able to stand with one foot in society at large and one foot in our own Church community. This is why Catholic thinkers have played such a significant role in determining public policy (for example, Father John A. Ryan, a Catholic theologian, who was instrumental in developing the concept of minimum wage, or Monsignor George Higgins, who has written widely on labor relations in our own time).[1]

Some Catholics today would like us to retreat into a smaller Church, one that would "mind its own business" and avoid involvement in political and social issues. But fortunately, our own common-sense moral tradition, based on natural law, human fulfillment, and reason, will not easily allow us to do that. Because we believe that society and nature are suffused with grace, and that reason enables all people of goodwill to discover that grace in human fulfillment, we are bound to discover what we can of God's plan for us even in a pluralistic society.

The Bible As a Source of Moral Wisdom

As the revealed word of God, the Bible holds a place of privilege in Christian ethics. Along with experience and reason, it provides us with a third source of moral wisdom. Yet there are different ways of using Scripture to arrive at moral decisions, some more fruitful than others. Let us look at several possibilities.

As a graduate student, I used to walk along the same route to school each day. Most days there was a car parked on the street that had a bumper sticker that read, "God said it, I believe it, that settles it." That bumper sticker, which reflects a more-or-less fundamentalist approach to Scripture, seems to imply that God has all the answers and makes them directly available to us in the Bible. It implies that all we need to do is consult it, and we will be able to find the answers to any moral problem that faces us. It suggests that Scripture alone can be our moral guide, without recourse to any other sources of moral wisdom, and perhaps even that God has not revealed moral wisdom any place other than in the pages of Scripture.

Catholics would find this understanding of the Bible unfamiliar, especially in moral matters. Unlike our Protestant brothers and sisters, we have not historically been accustomed to frequent contact with the

Bible, though happily there is a great surge of interest in Bible study among Catholics today. This renewed interest is due in part to the urging of Vatican Council II that Catholics "immerse themselves in Scripture," and to the *Catechism,* which encourages frequent reading of Scripture. While we certainly hold the Bible in esteem, Catholics have historically tended to prefer the dramatic and ritual enactment of the mysteries of salvation through our sacraments, art, and liturgy rather than only through the spoken or written word. Similarly, our moral tradition is based not primarily upon Scripture but upon reflecting about human nature and reasoning about what truly fulfills human nature. For us, morality is what makes us truly and fully happy in the long run, a fact that is largely verifiable by our experience. If that is so, then we might legitimately ask what the role of Scripture is in moral decision making. Is it merely icing on the cake, or does it serve as an important source of wisdom for us?

Various Uses of Scripture in Morality

The bumper sticker I used to see reflects one way in which we might use the Bible as a source of moral wisdom. Another is proof-texting, a cut-and-paste exercise in which we arrive at a decision on a particular issue and then seek supporting evidence for it from Scripture. This is relatively easy since the Bible is large and has ambiguous or conflicting statements that can be used to support many different moral choices. Nazi Germans appealed to Scripture to support their genocide, nineteenth-century Americans used it to uphold slavery, and many today claim to find support in it for separation of the races.

At the opposite extreme are those who deny any relevance at all to the scriptural witness. They feel that since the words of Scripture were written so long ago, for other audiences, they cannot possibly have anything to say to us. Unlike those who see perfect agreement between scriptural times and our own age, these people feel that the historical changes that have taken place since the Bible was written are so dramatic that they render the Bible useless to us in modern times.

A final approach, which most closely characterizes the Catholic understanding, is that Scripture has priority as one important source of moral wisdom but that by itself it is inadequate to provide moral norms.

This is true for a number of reasons, namely, that the Bible as a source of moral wisdom is incomplete, is not fully in agreement internally, and must be interpreted.

Incompleteness

Although the biblical witness is lengthy and complex, there are many contemporary moral issues that it does not treat. The question of *in vitro* fertilization, for example, finds no scriptural treatment at all and could not have been envisioned by the pretechnical mind-set of biblical writers. Similarly, questions of organ transplantation or the withdrawal of hydration and nutrition from seriously ill patients who are being maintained by artificial means find no resolution in Scripture. And even though the Bible has something to say about war, in no way could it have anticipated the advent of chemical or nuclear weapons, which clearly present a new moral situation.

Lack of Unity

In other cases, Scripture addresses problems or moral questions, but with conflicting evidence. Many passages in the Old Testament, for example, seem to extol the glory of war as a sign of God's protective favor to the Israelites. In the New Testament, it is written that Jesus himself said that he came not "to bring peace, but a sword" (Matthew 10:34); elsewhere, he reminded the disciples that they might need their swords (Luke 22:36). Yet other passages seem starkly to contradict these. In Matthew 26:52, Jesus said that those "who take the sword will perish by the sword" (Matthew 26:52); and more than once he urged people to do good to those who persecuted them, or to "turn the other cheek and offer no resistance." Over the centuries both the just-war theory (which allowed the use of violence if certain criteria were met) and pacifism (which eschewed all violence as inappropriate to Christians) found support in these Scriptural passages. Today, both are legitimate options for Christians.

In the matter of wealth and poverty, it is written in one place that Jesus said his disciples should "sell all they have," and that it is "more difficult for a rich man to enter the kingdom of heaven than for a camel to pass through the eye of a needle." Yet elsewhere he used the parable of the talents to suggest that we should be wise in our investments.

Interpretation

Even when Scripture does treat of a particular moral issue, and does so without apparent contradiction, there is still the problem of understanding what the writer meant. Some passages, like the Ten Commandments, are relatively clear and easy to understand, but they are also very general. It is also important to remember that at least the last seven commandments (honor thy father and mother, do not steal, do not lie, and so on) are also part of the natural law; that is, they reflect basic human values that can be discovered by reason without the help of revelation. Any reasonable person, even one without religious faith, can conceivably understand that killing, lying, and adultery are wrong.

Other passages are more troublesome. In one crucial passage relating to the permissibility of divorce, for example, the text of Matthew says that divorce is permissible only in some cases:

> Whoever divorces his wife, except for unchastity, and marries another commits adultery (Matthew 19:9).

But it is not clear whether one word, translated elsewhere as "lewd conduct," means unchastity, incest, or adultery. The problem is further complicated by the fact that in his gospel the writer of Mark quoted Jesus as saying, "Whoever divorces his wife and marries another commits adultery against her" (Mark 10:11) and did not mention the exception found in Matthew. To this day, Catholics hold that divorce is never permissible, and that the passages refer only to the permissibility of separation without remarriage and not to divorce as such. Over the centuries the Church has chosen to interpret the vague and conflicting scriptural evidence in this way because the scriptural answer itself is not crystal clear.

How Is the Bible Useful for Morality?

Given these problems of history and interpretation, is the Bible useless to us in answering moral questions? Far from it, if we understand the purpose of the Bible. It is important to remember that there are a number of levels of moral teaching ranging from very specific moral laws to more general attitudes, values, and goals. While the Bible responds to all of them, it is more useful at some levels than at others. A number of writers, including James Gustafson, William Spohn, and Lisa Cahill, have described these levels in various ways. One way of summarizing them would be as follows.

Laws and Specific Decisions

Morality has largely to do with specific decisions in particular situations, and many times these decisions are guided by laws that tell us what to do. The Bible does contain specific moral laws (such as those found in Leviticus 14, which described how the priest was to offer sacrifice and purify lepers), but as we have already shown, there are many other important moral questions that are not covered at all. So we might say that the Bible has some relevance at the level of specific laws and decisions, but it is not a reference book in which we can find all the answers. An example is found in Paul's letter to the Romans, in which Paul addressed a particular church community and referred to dietary requirements that are no longer binding for us:

> Welcome those who are weak in faith, but not for the purpose of quarreling over opinions. Some believe in eating anything, while the weak eat only vegetables…(14:1–2).

Paul was here alluding to a very specific moral law, but it is so specific to the time and culture of the first-century church that it seems irrelevant to us.

Moral Norms

Moral norms are more general than moral laws and could be addressed to any believing community. Again, from Paul as he wrote to the Romans:

> Owe no one anything, except to love one another; for the one who loves another has fulfilled the law (13:8).

At this level, the scriptural word is more general, but it yields more information than it would if we were looking for specific moral laws relating to specific situations.

Values, Goals, and Ideals

Values, goals, and ideals are the concrete goods-to-be-sought. They are the basis for both moral laws and moral norms, and without them moral laws would be completely arbitrary. They provide the "why" for moral teachings. Unity, friendship, community togetherness, and care for one another are all reasons why Paul exhorted the Romans to love and tolerate those who were weak in faith. Although eating meat sacrificed to idols is no longer an issue for us today, we still seek the values and ideals of Church community that Paul held so dear and tried to demonstrate to the early Church.

The Bible and Christian Character

The scriptural writers were interested in laws, norms, and ideals. But they were even more interested in forming a people. Their message, which contained God's own call to be the people of God, was spoken to shape the Jews, and later Christians, into the chosen people who would exhibit certain kinds of characteristics. So while Scripture is sometimes helpful in telling us what kinds of choices we should make, it is far more helpful in teaching us what kinds of persons we should be.

In the Catholic tradition, answers to specific questions are usually reasoned out from available knowledge about human nature and community. We do not look to the Bible for answers about genetic engineering, for example; rather, we ask, "What does it mean to be human?" and from that we deduce God's purpose in creating us and try to discover the extent to which we might alter our genetic makeup. Instead of providing concrete answers to detailed scientific questions such as these, the Bible forms our attitudes, values, and character, shaping us into disciples—persons who think clearly and lovingly about the moral questions that we face. Scripture does not contradict human moral wisdom but illuminates the norms we arrive at through reason, making them clearer and more appealing.

Christians should allow themselves to be bathed in the word of Scripture. Looking to Scripture for specific answers is not bad, but it can be frustrating and at odds with the reasons for which the evangelists or prophets originally wrote. Through its liturgy, the Church provides exposure to a significant portion of the scriptural word. The readings we hear at Mass on Sundays and weekdays give us long segments of the four evangelists, Paul, and the Hebrew Scriptures. The point is not to give us a moral textbook but to relate the Christian story from many different perspectives so that our understanding of it becomes fuller over the years. Personal study of Scripture enhances our appreciation of it and helps make us true disciples who make good moral choices. Gradually, our moral sense is trained by these words, so that we come to choose well naturally and easily.

Theologians who study Scripture for its moral message know that it is important to see Scripture as a whole, to respect the kind of writing any particular passage represents, and to take careful account of the historical and cultural setting in which the passage was written. The poetry of the psalms, for example, must be understood in a different light from that of the admonitions of Paul to his early Church communities, which were written centuries later and for different reasons.

Preaching and the Moral Life

Paul asked the Romans, "How will they hear unless someone preaches?" Preaching makes the biblical word come to life, and it is also the Church's way of leading us into a fuller experience of grace and of shaping our moral lives. Unfortunately, preaching on morality has gotten a bad name because of "fire and brimstone" sermons that scold and berate people. Good preaching helps us see our sins, but it should also lead us to see our lives in a different light, to do something concrete as a result of our faith, and to show us how to find the happiness that is the heart of morality. Good preachers use the scriptural word not only to show us where we have fallen short, but to illuminate the grace in our lives and make us thirst for a greater portion of it.

Preaching is not just a lecture. It can be described as a persuasive conversation that involves the preacher, the Word of God, and the congregation. It requires that the preacher understand the scriptural word, preach from faith and humility, and use rhetorical and communication skills to move us to action. Preaching should move us to reform our personal lives, and it should bring the Church as a whole into deeper dialogue with society on important social issues.

Because of our love for the liturgy, art, and music of the Church, Catholics sometimes neglect the importance of preaching. In addition to studying Scripture ourselves, we should also expect our priests to preach conscientiously on the biblical texts, relating them carefully to the moral issues we all face in our daily lives. Preachers must look first to the moral issues that surround us (the morning paper is a good place to start) and then ask, "What do today's Scripture readings have to say to this issue?" After having taught a course entitled "Preaching on Moral Issues" for several years, I am convinced that any set of readings can yield an effective word on any moral issue that faces us.

Yves Congar, the great theologian of Vatican Council II who was made a cardinal by Pope John Paul II in 1994, once said that if there were two countries, one that had only preaching and the other that had only the Eucharist, faith would be stronger in that country with only preaching.[2] This suggests how important preaching is to the spiritual, moral, and liturgical life of the Church. Priests and others who preach must take their responsibility much more seriously and allow sufficient time for study, prayer, and reflection on the biblical word.

The responsibility for preaching is shared by those in the pews, too. They must let the preacher know that they listen to what he or she says, and they must be active participants in the act of preaching. No preacher can alone carry the burden of making God's word come alive. Those of us who hear preaching must listen attentively, offer critique and comment, and make the dialogue that goes on between priest and congregation a strong and vital one.

For Further Reading

Spohn, William, S.J. *What Are They Saying about Scripture and Ethics?* Mahwah, N.J.: Paulist, 1983.

Part 2

THE HEART OF
CATHOLIC MORALITY

Chapter 4

Conscience As
Our Moral Compass

We have explored how experience, reason, and Scripture all serve us as we approach specific moral decisions. Conscience uses them all. Conscience is the human capacity, at once a kind of "moral vision," or "compass," and a judgment, that enables us to relate experience, reason, and Scripture to the particular problem that faces us.

The U.S. government has what is sometimes referred to as its "conscience fund." Over the years, people, usually anonymously, send checks to this fund to make good on unpaid taxes, thefts, or other injustices that are sometimes never even specified. The fund receives hundreds of thousands of dollars each year, and each receipt signals that someone has rethought the moral implications of something done in the past—one might say that people returning the money had "guilty consciences," or that their "consciences were bothering them."

Such statements would reflect one common understanding of conscience: it is a "feeling" that won't leave us alone, that tries to tell us that we have either done something wrong or failed to do something we should have done.

Another way we often understand *conscience* is as something that is in opposition to the law. Someone who deliberately violates the law, for example, is sometimes called a "conscientious objector." We occasionally read of highly conscientious people who deliberately set out to be arrested by trespassing on private property to protest abortion, cross government lines to stage a "sit-in" at a plant that builds destructive weapons, or refuse to report when drafted for military duty. These cases suggest that sometimes conscience is at odds with the law or custom, and that we must either follow the law or follow our consciences.

Conscience As a "Warehouse of Values"

The reality of conscience is at once more complex and simpler than this. At one level, conscience is our basic awareness of good and evil. Each of us can probably recall a moment early in our lives when we first realized that some things are to be done merely because they are "right," while others are to be avoided because they are "wrong." Very young children do not have this ability—they do what they are told because "Mommy said so," or because they fear getting caught and punished. With the help of experience and parental guidance, however, children gradually move to the point of their "first moral act"—the first time they act not out of fear of punishment or obedience, but because they realize that stealing, lying, or cruelty are wrong and harmful. Whenever that moment comes (and most of us probably don't recall exactly when it was), we have the first spark of conscience. We have the first brick of what author Vincent Rush has called our "warehouse of values," the place where we "store" our moral knowledge, awareness, and sensitivity, to be drawn on all through the rest of our lives.[1]

Parents see this in their children and might be thrilled by the first time a child comes home from school and announces that even though she had stolen a toy from a playmate, she had come to realize that it was bad to do that and had returned the toy. Rudimentary as it seems, this is the first time the child has understood what "good" and "evil" are, and the first time the child has made an authentic moral choice.

Some persons' "warehouses" of values are vast and well-stocked, while other people never seem to develop one at all. Others develop values and goals that seem warped and disoriented. The movie *Silence of the Lambs*, for example, focuses on a psychopathic killer named Hannibal Lecter; he is highly intelligent, yet because of mental illness has no apparent awareness of the moral value of human life. Though imprisoned, he escapes and repeatedly performs vicious acts of mutilation and murder. These acts horrify us and are clearly the product of a sick mind; but they are also extreme examples of what happens when a person lacks moral values to shape the decisions he or she makes.

But conscience is more than just moral awareness, or a place where we keep our moral values. It is also practical: that is, it must come to bear on practical decisions about what is to be done here and now. It is not just something hidden away in the recesses of our minds but something that must shape our decisions and our lives. We must make practical, specific decisions about many different things: whether to repay a loan or take office supplies from the company for which we work; whether to engage in sex with someone to whom we are not married; whether to try to achieve conception by some means of *in vitro* fertilization; whether to continue medical treatments "at all costs" or to forgo some, even though it might mean that our lives (or those for whom we are making decisions) are shortened.

Conscience As an Ability to Choose

In these concrete instances, conscience takes on a different character. It is no longer just a set of values and goals, or a vague "feeling" that prompts us to "feel guilty" about something we have done or might do, but rather a hard-nosed, careful judgment about what we must do. Should I cheat on my taxes and use the money to pay my child's tuition? Should I miss Mass in favor of visiting a sick friend? Should I give to this charity or that, or to none at all? Should I persevere in a difficult and abusive marriage, or abandon it for my own health and perhaps the good of my children? Should I undergo this difficult and painful medical treatment, with some small hope that it will make me better, or should I use my remaining days to prepare myself spiritually?

Decisions of conscience like this are not easy because they rarely present us with two stark alternatives, one good and one evil. Almost inevitably, we are presented with two goods: the good of money for tuition versus the good of civic duty to pay taxes; the good of the spiritual benefit of Mass versus the needs of a sick friend; the good of fidelity in marriage versus my (or my children's) psychological and spiritual welfare; the good of sexual pleasure and enjoyment versus the good of faithfulness, wholeness, and honesty. So rather than having merely good and evil to choose from, conscience, as a judgment, must choose carefully among many different goods and must often find a balance among them. For this reason, the exercise of conscience is really a skill that we acquire over a lifetime. Far from being just a feeling that arises involuntarily from within us, conscience is a highly developed awareness of moral good and evil as well as an act of judgment about how that moral good is to be realized in this particular instance.

Conscience is complex, but it can be described in three basic steps: deliberation, decision, and action.

Deliberation

Deliberation is primarily a matter of gathering information and establishing options about the choices before us. It is the most detailed of the three steps, and itself has several parts. The first step of deliberation is seeing reality as it is since, like a captain piloting a ship in the fog, we cannot make good decisions about things we cannot see. I am reminded of the story of a priest who was about to have surgery to remove his appendix. After carefully explaining the procedure to him, the surgeon asked if he understood what was going to happen. The priest assured the surgeon he did, but had one question: "Will the scar show above my collar?" Obviously, the priest didn't see the reality of the surgery very well and was not prepared to make a good decision about it. A judgment of conscience begins with a clear understanding of the question we face.

A second dimension of deliberation is consultation, or seeking the opinion and expertise of those around us. We do this not only because other people may have wisdom we do not possess (especially in technical matters, such as those relating to healthcare) but also because our decisions have social implications that affect other people. We sometimes think of morality as a "private matter" that does not concern others, but it is a rare moral choice that has absolutely no implications for someone else. Even choices relating to sexual conduct, which we usually consider to be personal, can have vast social consequences if the choice results in destabilizing a marriage or spreading a sexually transmitted disease.

Consulting others can also be a helpful way of avoiding excessive self-interest or prejudice that may affect our judgment. Even when we try to be objective, our self-interest and subjectivity can get in the way of a good decision. I am reminded of a man who came to see me about a relationship he was having with a woman who worked in his office. Although the relationship had grown to involve sexual intimacy, he was shocked when I used the word "adultery." "It isn't adultery," he said with a hurt look on his face. But as we discussed it, his vision became clearer, and he admitted he hadn't wanted to see it as adultery because the relationship had been so rewarding for him. Just as we ask a lawyer's advice before deciding whether to file a lawsuit, so in many moral decisions we should consult those whose opinions and moral maturity and objectivity we respect.

Another dimension of deliberation is memory. When we face moral decisions, there are often events in our own past that can put a helpful light on the situation at hand. As we deliberate, we should always search our own experience to see if anything similar has happened in the past, and if so, what alternatives, consequences, and possibilities existed at the time. Although our ability to do this is limited when we are young (which is why we sometimes say that experience is the best teacher), as we grow older, our remembrances grow, too, and we have more and more wisdom and experience upon which to draw.

"Remembering" also involves Church tradition and teaching, since this is the body of accumulated wisdom passed on from one age to another. This is why Church teaching plays such an important role in decisions of conscience. Sometimes we hear people say, "I had to decide whether to follow the Church's teaching or follow my conscience"—but this is a false dichotomy. It is rarely a question of having to choose one over another, but rather of allowing conscience to use Church teaching as it uses other kinds of memory to inform choice. Church teaching on a particular matter may not always provide us with an exact answer to a specific question, but it tells us far more than we can know on our own as individuals because it reaches back through centuries of Christian experience. Church tradition in moral matters functions like a road sign: it points us in a direction and helps us get where we are going. There may be detours or exceptional cases along the way, but generally the Church's wisdom should weigh heavily in the moral decisions we make. We should depart from it regretfully and only after prayerful deliberation.

Decision

When we have finished the process of deliberation, we must eventually decide—that is, determine how to achieve the best possible balance of good in a particular case. After we have looked carefully at the choices before us, taken counsel, and remembered both our own experience and that of the Church, we must decide what to do, since in the last analysis conscience is a practical function—it always leads to a decision.

Emotions are important here, too. Sometimes emotions can be detrimental to good decision making—for instance if we are so angry that we "can't see straight." But emotions always play some role in deciding, and we must listen to them. If we "feel," for example, that a proposed course of action is wrong, we must take that into account because sometimes our emotions "know" moral goodness or evil before we apprehend it with our minds. As human persons we have feelings as well as reason and will, and all three of these must come into play as we decide. And when we make a moral decision that is felt and reasoned and willed all at once, we use all our human ability and make a fully human decision.

Action

Although it may seem obvious, action is the final stage of conscience. Once we have deliberated and decided what ought to be done, we must do it. When we fail to follow through, we sin, for we know what is to be done, yet we fail to act.

Taken together, these steps represent what we mean by the "formation of conscience." Our conscience is one of our human abilities, and we train it just as we train our brains or our muscles. A "bad conscience" or a "lazy conscience" is one that has been trained poorly: it does not have an adequate store of values, it does not know how to deliberate, it can't come to a decision, or it lacks the courage to act. Whenever these defects are voluntary, they involve sin, because they reflect an unwillingness "to do the right thing."

Our conscience is our moral vision. It is the only way we can see the moral reality before us and the only way we can choose. This is why courts sometimes hold hearings to determine whether a person accused of a crime is "competent to stand trial." What the court really wants to know is whether this person understands good and evil and has the ability to choose. In short, the court is asking, "Does this person's conscience function well enough to bear responsibility for a crime?"

Because our conscience is the only way we can see morally, we are bound to follow our judgment of conscience even when it is in error. If I deliberate, decide, and act with sincerity and good intention, I am "bound" by that choice. This is why some persons, during war, conclude that war is immoral and refuse to fight, despite public pressure, legal censures, and even prison terms. So even when our decisions are at odds with Church teaching, if they are fully conscientious and sincere, we must follow them. When we depart from Church tradition, from counsel given by others, or from our own past experience, we are getting further and further out on a limb. But if we take the steps of choice as carefully as we can, appropriating the moral values before us as fully as we know how, we can trust our conscience as a faithful friend who will help us see—and choose—clearly and rightly.

For Further Reading

Gula, Richard. *Reason Informed by Faith.* Mahwah, N.J.: Paulist, 1989. Chapters 9, 10, 11.

O'Connell, Timothy. *Principles For A Catholic Morality,* revised edition. New York: Crossroad, 1990. Chapter 9, "Conscience."

Rush, Vincent. *The Responsible Christian.* Chicago: Loyola University Press, 1984. Chapter 5.

Chapter 5

Fundamental Choices for Good and Evil

In the recent movie *The Age of Innocence* we see the lushly portrayed story of a young man and woman set against the background of high society and its rigid mores and class structure in late-nineteenth-century New York. The film focuses on a young man, played by Jeremy Irons, and an expatriate divorcée, played by Michelle Pfeiffer. In the course of the movie, their deep love for each other blossoms passionately, but only in the subtle gestures allowed by the times. Both of them are bound: she by her marginal status as a divorcée, he by his betrothal to another woman whom he does not truly love, but who has the proper social status. The movie is an intense, passionate study of moral character and highlights the importance of choice. To the very end of the movie, one is not sure which choice the couple will make: will they indulge their love for each other and shatter previous commitments, or will they choose to forgo their mutual satisfaction and remain apart?

Though set in a time whose strictures and formalities seem foreign to us, *The Age of Innocence* reminds us of how crucial choices are to our lives, and of how often choices must be made again and again to retain their validity. It also shows how our ability to choose well is limited—or enhanced—by external forces.

Although it seems an unlikely and incongruous sequel, Pope John Paul II's recent encyclical *The Splendor of Truth* (*Veritatis Splendor,* August, 1993) is really about choice as well. In the opening paragraphs of his letter, the pope noted that choice is our way of responding to God and the meaning of life itself. The call to make those choices—that is, the call to morality—"deeply touches every person," even those who do not have religious faith. None of us can live a human life and not ask, "What ought I to do?" The answer may be found in religious or nonreligious terms, but we can avoid it only by living a completely irresponsible life.

The "Problem" of Freedom

God created us free. We have the ability to know good and evil, and we may choose evil (often under the guise of a very short term good) if we so desire. Although this freedom is one of the most distinctive marks of what it means to be human, it is also problematic.

Columnist William Pfaff has noted that Americans embrace a kind of radically individual freedom, a freedom from restraints, a freedom that allows us to do whatever we want from one moment to the next.[1] On the left, he has said, this is characterized by radical personal choice (for example, to organize protests, have abortions, or refuse military service), on the right by economic individualism and market freedom (for example, insistence on low taxes, minimal governmental involvement, and few social services).

The pope's encyclical, on the other hand, maintains that while there is indeed freedom from interference and control, there must also be freedom *to:* freedom to make choices and to become certain kinds of persons. The exquisite tension of *The Age of Innocence,* for example, comes not only from the free choice that faces the two lovers—that is, whether they will take this or that action here and now—but also the choice about who they are to be. True moral deliberation takes into account not only what we choose to do, but who we choose to be, and the two are intimately related.

One of the primary points of the encyclical was to address this issue. The pope raised the question of the "fundamental option" and rightly criticized any understanding of it that separates this "freedom to do" from "freedom to be." Drawing on the gospel story of the rich young man, he wrote that the question the man faced was not just about "rules to be followed, but about the full meaning of life" (#7). Although distinct, these two kinds of choices cannot be separated without risking our "substantial integrity or personal unity" (#67). "We create ourselves" by our moral choices (#71); we cannot do one thing and be another. If I choose to tell a lie, I risk becoming a liar. If I cheat once, I become untrustworthy. The characters in *The Age of Innocence* agonize over whether they can express their love, but even more they worry about what such a choice will do to them as persons.

It is also important to recall, as is so apparent in *The Age of Innocence*, that our free choices are never entirely private and personal. Just as choosing to express their love for each other will have wide repercussions among those around these movie characters, so all of our "free" choices must take others into account. We are radically free, but human freedom, the only kind we know, is also freedom-in-community, whether that be family, city, or world.

What We Know and How We Know It

A second important part of *Veritatis Splendor* was to ask how much we are able to know about morality or human fulfillment. Is there any objective, a once-and-for-all dimension to this "meaning of life"? Are there real, tangible choices that realize it, and others that are absolutely at odds with it? Or is my grasp of this meaning as personal and unique as my fingerprint? Is there no way to verify whether I have chosen well?

While the pope fully acknowledged the importance of subjective factors and circumstances that make my life and my moral choices different from everyone else's, he stressed that there is a "moral order," that is, a way things ought to be, and that there are certain choices that are always at odds with this order, choices that are "intrinsically evil." This is a difficult term. To many people, it seems to describe an act that is really, really disobedient. But at its root, it means an act that by its nature offends who we are as persons. It is not wrong just because someone else says so; it is wrong because it hurts me.

In a commentary on the encyclical, *New York Times* writer Peter Steinfels used rape as one example of intrinsic evil.[2] Rape is wrong, Steinfels wrote, not only "because it offends one's conscience or because society has forbidden it." Rather, it is wrong because it violates the very nature of humanity. It is a fundamental violation of the victim's personhood, and of the perpetrator's human dignity as well. Rape, murder for hire, and gross injustice are fundamentally inhuman acts: they are evil in kind and cannot be justified by any good intention nor mitigated by any circumstances. Even if some very good result were to come of it (for example, the freedom of an innocent person from a death camp), we would still say that rape as a means to obtain it is inherently wrong. It has, as Steinfels wrote, "evil built into its character," so its moral character is not just "pasted on" but rooted in what the act means: violence, assault, and coercion. Undertaking an intrinsically evil act, therefore, is far more than being really disobedient; it is a question of doing something fundamentally at odds with what it means to be human.

Although there is debate among theologians as to which acts are intrinsically evil, and about how our understanding of them can develop with our understanding of the human person (slavery, for example, was not always seen as intrinsically evil because slaves were not understood as having souls), the encyclical is clear in stating that careful reflection will reveal these abiding truths to us.

How Do We Know?

How do we discover these inherent moral qualities? The second part of the encyclical addressed this question and answered it primarily in terms of natural law (as discussed in chapter 3). This term is often confused with "the laws of nature," which have to do with animal instincts and physics. Natural law, a rational awareness of the order of creation, reveals that God created us as one thing and not another, and that this has certain moral implications. If I were to make a vacuum cleaner, for example, which has one purpose, it would certainly have different operating instructions than a telephone, which has quite a different purpose. All the more for humans, whom God created as rational, feeling creatures who live in community. There are certain acts that are just incompatible with being human, just as there are certain things you cannot do to a vacuum cleaner or a phone. But unlike household appliances, human persons can reflect on who they are and what their purpose is, and in that reflection discover the natural law.

The encyclical states that natural law is not just a question of "obedience to an external authority" (#41), nor is it only a set of propositions (#88) or mere norms on a biological level (#50). Rather, it is an exercise in reason by which we discover God's eternal plan "implanted in beings endowed with reason, and inclining them *toward the right action and end*" (#44). Not imposed on us like an authoritarian law, natural law is a "participation in God's providence" (#43); as creatures who can think, we are actually able to think like God "thinks," and to some extent know what God wishes for us.

Far from restrictive or coercive, natural law is an ever-expanding, reasoned awareness of what human life should be. Most important, because natural law is a function of reason, it is available to every reasoning person, believer or not. This is why the pope's encyclical received such widespread attention from the press. It was not speaking only of narrow, religious beliefs but of the deep, resounding truths of human nature. Not all reasoning persons will immediately agree on what constitutes the fully human, but the importance of the pope's message is that fundamental agreement is possible, at least on basic moral questions pertaining to life itself, justice, and the proper use of our bodies.

The Role of Scripture

The encyclical emphasizes the centrality of reason and natural law, which are the foundations of Catholic morality. The simplicity and universality of this approach in a pluralistic society in which many do not share our religious views is obvious. Saying that abortion, lack of housing, or artificial insemination are wrong because they are against the law of God is persuasive to believers, but not to those who do not believe. Using natural law to show that these acts are irrational because they are at odds with what it means to be human will give Catholics a voice even in the most diverse society.

But despite the importance of natural law, the pope began his encyclical with a long homily on the gospel story of the rich young man who approached Jesus and asked him what he must do to be saved. In his long explanation of this passage (which, by the way, is a good model for pastors who might want to preach on moral questions), the pope used the rich young man as a symbol for all of us who have the same question. This explication of the story's symbolism demonstrates that Scripture is an important source for our moral decisions, too, and that we should use it in conjunction with natural law in shaping our lives. While natural law may provide the rational basis for our choices, Scripture provides the heart, the spirit, and the internal motivation. Just as Jesus gently called the rich young man to follow him as a disciple, the same call is extended to us through our personal meditation on Scripture, our Bible study, good preaching, and our participation in liturgy. It does not replace what we know by reason but fulfills it and brings it to life.

Is This Encyclical for Me?

Recently, as I participated in a symposium on the encyclical, one of the priests in the audience asked, "What are the implications of this for me, as a pastor?" I told him these are the questions moral theologians are afraid someone will ask because they force us to come down to earth and "make sense of it all."

Veritatis Splendor is addressed to the bishops, yet it is obviously intended as guidance for all of us.

There are at least three central points of abiding importance for all of us.

1. Morality is more than obedience and authority. While the pope speaks as an authentic moral teacher, he teaches that there is a moral order, a "way-things-ought-to-be" that is built into human nature. We discover—not create—it. Although the process by which we discover these values is an active participation in God's own mind, it does lead to a definite kind of human fulfillment. We are not adrift on a sea of equally valid choices.

2. The moral life is cumulative; that is, it adds up. Rather than making one-choice-for-all, or a series of choices that have no connection, our moral lives involve many choices (like those in *The Age of Innocence*) that build us up as moral agents and give us character. This is the satisfying part of morality, when we realize that we have begun to "make something of ourselves." Moral wisdom involves learning from our mistakes, doing

better next time, and savoring the small victories of commitment, fidelity, compassion, truthfulness, and wholeness that we achieve by grace.

3. The Church has something to say to the world at large. It was amazing how much attention the encyclical received from the secular press. All national newspapers and magazines covered it, and one commentator referred to it as an "Encyclical for Everyman." This shows that the Church, for all its problems, remains a strong and influential voice in the world.

Although the encyclical is long and technical, it does provide an incentive to priests to preach more effectively on moral issues (both by opening questions and shaping answers); to scholars and teachers to explore this objective "meaning of life" with students; and to all of us to look carefully for the moral questions that surround us each day. In so doing we will come to see the moral life not as a burden or an oppression but as an exciting opportunity to shape our future, our society, and ourselves.

For Further Reading

Allsop, Michael and John O'Keefe, eds. *Veritatis Splendor: American Responses.* Kansas City, Mo.: Sheed & Ward, 1995.

Wilkins, John, ed. *Considering Veritatis Splendor.* Cleveland, Ohio: The Pilgrim Press, 1994.

Chapter 6

Whatever Happened to Sin?

In the movie *White Palace*, Susan Sarandon plays a waitress who works in a hamburger stand in downtown St. Louis. Although raised Catholic, she falls in love with a wealthy Jewish lawyer from the suburbs, and the plot of the movie revolves around the disparity of their backgrounds. At one point her friend asks her about her religion. "I used to be Catholic," she says, "but confession made me jumpy."

A lot of Catholics today could probably echo that sentiment. While confession was once a staple and an identifying characteristic of Catholicism, it has seen a rapid decline in recent years. This has made many people worry that sin has disappeared. Many parents worry that their children do not value confession as they did, and see this as necessarily a bad sign. But before we answer the question of confession, let's look a little more closely at the reality of sin itself.

The traditional definition of mortal sin is that it is an act that involves serious matter chosen freely with full knowledge and assent of the will. More simply put, to commit a sin we have to be free of coercion and pressure, know that we are doing something wrong, and still choose to do it. It is important to remember, however, that sin, even though it involves evil, is never a direct choice of evil. No rational person chooses something completely evil, and there is always something about the choice that at least appears good. Sin is more a lack of something that ought to be there than a choice of a positive bad thing. It might be said to be the choice of a good, but of a very limited good.

Sin As Disobedience

There are a number of ways in which we can look at sin. One popular way is to understand sin as "breaking the law of God," or "disobeying God," such as when we violate one of the Ten Commandments. Many of us learned a kind of "examination of conscience" based on the Ten Commandments. To prepare for confession we asked ourselves whether we had taken the Lord's name in vain, disobeyed our parents, had impure thoughts, and so on. While sinful acts do involve breaking the law, however, this is not an adequate understanding of sin because it easily lends itself to legalism, that is, to saying that "morality" is equal to "obeying the law." The weakness of this thinking is apparent if we consider for a moment the fact that one can obey the letter of the law while ignoring or even abusing its spirit. Someone may, for example, "obey" the law that prohibits the charging of excessive interest on a loan, but at the same time abuse the intent of that law by adding "service charges" that are really the equivalent of higher interest.

Sin As Relational

Another way in which we might understand sin is in terms of relationship—that is, we see our relationship with God as one of friendship, or love, and sin as a weakening or a break in that relationship. In this case, sinning is like offending a good friend. The trust and the joy of the relationship is weakened or destroyed. In more traditional terms, we distinguish between "mortal" and "venial" sins. Mortal sins are those that involve offenses so serious that they kill the relationship with God altogether, putting us in a "state of sin," out of communion or friendship with God. Venial sins, on the other hand, are those that weaken the relationship to God but do not entirely destroy it, just as forgetting a luncheon engagement with a friend might cause offense, but would not have the same effect on the friendship as stealing or lying or slander.

This relational view has great appeal to us today because our society is absorbed in the importance of relationships. In many ways, our society and our view of life is highly psychologized, and our relationships with others—and the things that make them better or worse—are central to our experience. Another advantage of this view is that it reminds us that God is a person, and that we may "fall in love" with God just as we fall in love with other humans. Understanding sin as a weakening of that love relationship has many parallels in our own lives, and it helps us see that sin is not just an act against a law but an act against a person who loves us. In this model, the sacrament of reconciliation does not merely "absolve" us of sin but helps heal the rift that has occurred because of our offense.

Sin As Choice of a Limited Good

Yet another way of seeing sin is to regard it as the choice of a short-term good over a longer-term good. This view makes sense if we accept that no rational person chooses pure evil—there is always some apparent good that is the object of choice. The employee who embezzles from her company, for example, does not make a choice for the absolute evil of theft; in her mind, she is choosing the good of economic security for herself or her family, or perhaps the acquisition of certain things that will make life more pleasant. Perhaps she even sees her act as rectifying the injustice of the low wages she has received over the years. In another case, a physician may recommend a procedure he knows may not be in the patient's best interest. He does so not to choose evil for the patient but to choose the short-term good of financial gain, professional prestige (perhaps for perfecting an experimental procedure), or enhancement of his skills. None of these things is evil in itself, but when they are chosen over the greater goods of professional integrity, trust, and the commitment of the medical profession to always act in the patient's best interest, they can be seen as sin.

Television ads sometimes tell us that we should "be all that we can be." Sin is a deliberate choice to be less than we can be: less honest, less caring, less truthful, less whole. Sin means choosing for the moment when we know that there are much longer term goods or goals to be sought. Sometimes this is just plain old selfishness: we can't overcome the temptation to choose what is good for me rather than what is good for us. Other times it is a deliberate unwillingness to discover what the long-term goods are.

There are two important things to remember about sin. First, sin is not merely acting but becoming. Each time we sin—whether we see it as a disobedient act, an unloving act, or an act that favors a short-term over a long-term good—we affect who we are as persons. The fact that Catholic theology always speaks not only of sins but of a "state of sin," or "vice," reminds us that our acts shape who we are. When we witness a co-worker or friend lie on several occasions, for example, we begin to make a judgment about that person's character or moral identity: we begin to wonder if he or she is a liar. And to call someone a liar is a much more radical moral judgment than merely to say that someone told a lie. Similarly, while one instance of sexual impropriety does not necessarily a degenerate make, repeated infidelities make us "easy," promiscuous, or worse. Our acts shape our character.

So sin exists on two levels: The level of acts, which can be disobedient, unloving, or lacking potential for fulfillment. And the level of character, for sin ultimately shapes who we are as persons. That is why it is important to ask ourselves repeatedly, "Does this act represent the kind of person I want to be?"

The second important thing about sin is that it is always a social act, that is, an act that affects those around us. Today it is fashionable to speak of a "right to privacy," which implies that certain actions have no real moral impact on family, society, or nation. But if we believe, as the Catholic moral tradition does, that people are inherently connected with one another, then very few of my acts are absolutely private and without social implications. And at some level, there is a further reality we call "social sin," which is the injustice that becomes "built in" to our laws, social customs, and structures. It is often tempting to say that we "can't do anything" about social problems that deprive people of rights or housing or employment; but we must always remember that it is persons who make laws and create structures, and that even though they become complex and entrenched, they can always be changed. So our responsibility extends not just to "doing good acts" ourselves, nor even to "becoming certain kinds of persons." It also involves doing whatever we can to assure that the society in which we live is just and equitable. We must be prudent, of course, about how much we can do to effect social change. But most of us can at least become informed about issues and vote intelligently, and that is a big step in the right direction.

We can even become aware of this social dimension of sin within our families. I once recommended to a married couple that they consider celebrating the sacrament of reconciliation together with a priest; they found the chance to speak their sins to each other, and to be reconciled to the Church and to each other, to be deeply fulfilling.

But confession remains a big problem for many of us. Some of us fear that the decline in the frequency of confession means that sin has disappeared and that no one takes sin seriously anymore. Others experience confession as a humiliating experience and welcome its demise.

But if we see sin as a choice of a lesser good and as a diminishment of who we are as persons, then confession becomes a kind of spiritual therapy. Far from being an encounter with an authority who judges us and "absolves" us of our sins, reconciliation becomes a therapeutic and healing moment when we face our own limitations and try to broaden our vision and choice so that we always choose the greatest good possible.

The decline in frequent confession may not be an entirely bad thing. Seeing confession as a time to recite a "laundry list" of sins week after week may trivialize sin and make it appear that we are just confessing little mistakes. If we go to confession somewhat less frequently, but with a deeper awareness of sin as a tendency, an inclination, and a state that needs to be healed, we might benefit more from it. Such an approach might help us remember that sin is not just "what we do" but "who we choose to become."

This healing does not happen all at once, and most of us will be plagued by the same sins—tendencies to choose the same short-term goods— over and over again. But confession provides us with the opportunity to face those limitations and to keep trying to "choose better," even if our choices improve only in fits and starts.

A wise therapist once told me that we should not expect therapy to turn us into different persons. If, for example, I look at myself as a strong solid oak tree, it would be unrealistic to expect myself to be transformed into a beautiful but fragile flowering magnolia. Similarly, reconciliation must aim at helping us be "better as who we are"—not changing radically overnight, but discovering our strengths, our best sides, and our gifts and allowing grace to enhance them. More like pruning and trimming than uprooting, confession should perfect what God has given us rather than destroy it.

For Further Reading

Donohoe, James. "Toward a Theology of Sin." *Church* (Spring 1986): 48–54.

McCormick, Patrick. *Sin As Addiction*. Mahwah, N.J.: Paulist, 1989.

O'Connell, Timothy. *Principles for a Catholic Morality*. New York: Harper and Row, 1990. Chapter 7, "The Theology of Sin" and chapter 8, "Sin: Mortal and Venial."

Chapter 7

Let Virtue Be Your Guide

V irtue," said Mark Twain, "has never been as respectable as money." What Twain was no doubt referring to is the fact that most of us find it easier to judge people on the basis of what they have or do than on the basis of who they are. People who amass huge fortunes or build large businesses or own impressive homes or cars earn a certain immediate respect from those they meet. Those whose material posses- sions or accomplishments are more modest but who are people of deep integrity, honesty, or compassion earn our respect much more slowly. Yet morality has far more to do with these latter qualities than with merely having or doing. How would I want others to describe me? As a person of great wealth, or as a person who is impeccably honest? As someone who has several thousand employees, or as someone known for justice and compassion?

We have already shown that through much of Christian history, morality was described primarily in terms of the virtues: flexible qualities of character that shape inclinations and dispositions to act in certain ways. At one point of history, the study of virtue was neglected in favor of a more legalistic approach to morality, which was concerned not so much with the cultivation of these qualities of character but with adherence to the law. Not that law is a bad thing. We need laws to guide us and show us the way. But morality and law are not the same thing. Law compels and directs from the outside, whereas morality (and virtue) grow from within, shaping the very core of who we are. This is evident from the fact that it is possible to keep the letter of the law while flagrantly and willfully violating its spirit. Take the example of a businessperson who scrupulously adheres to the state employment regulations but uses loopholes in the law to dismiss employees before they are eligible for pensions. As long as he or she stays within the requirements of the law, the employer cannot be accused of a crime, but we would certainly not consider him or her a person of sound moral character.

What Is Virtue?

Many years ago an article was written entitled "Virtue Is Not a Habit."[1] The title was ironic because properly understood, a habit is exactly what a virtue is. What the author of the article meant was that virtue is not a habit in the sense in which we usually understand the term, that is, as something we do unconsciously or involuntarily, like biting our fingernails or tapping our fingers on the desk, something of which we remain blissfully unaware until someone calls our attention to it. A moral habit (the word comes from the Latin word *habitus*) is any kind of activity that is consciously cultivated and nurtured until it becomes almost second nature. Quite unlike nervous, unconscious habits, moral habits are those skills that are developed over time, training our human capacities to respond readily and happily in a certain way. These moral habits are more like the ability acquired by athletes or musicians who practice for years at a time to be able to run a one-hundred-yard dash in record time or play a difficult piece of music flawlessly and gracefully.

Like musical or athletic skills, virtues can be strengthened by frequent use; they can also weaken or disintegrate through neglect. They enable our human capacities of desiring, willing, thinking, feeling, and judging to work together smoothly and to help us arrive at good moral decisions with ease. Let us take a look at four of the most important, or cardinal, virtues: temperance, fortitude, justice, and prudence.

Temperance: Frequently Sought, Seldom Achieved

Perhaps no virtue is more sought after today than temperance. Television and print ads reveal an almost obsessive concern with eating, drinking, and smoking too much. Dozens of plans promise to help us temper our desires for food, alcohol, or nicotine. What these programs promise, but seldom provide, is the virtue of temperance.

Temperance is the virtue related to our physical desires, especially those of touch. As such, temperance is the skill to moderate or train those desires. Although some advocates of temperance (the word is usually associated only with alcohol) have made it seem as though all desires "of the flesh" are sinful, in fact, temperance recognizes that these desires for physical pleasure and comfort are good. Our desire for good and beautiful things is at the very root of what morality means. But because of our human weakness, these desires must be properly trained. Temperance seeks the middle road: neither too much sensual gratification (which results in the vices of gluttony and lust), nor too little (which results in a vice Saint Thomas called insensibility—the inability to desire anything—a kind of moral anesthesia that blunts or destroys all our desires entirely). The excesses leave only the shell of a human person, someone unable to enjoy anything, even God. Temperance teaches us to enjoy beauty and comfort and physical pleasure, but in a measured way appropriate to how we live our lives. Like the other virtues, it is flexible. What is "just enough" for me may be too much or too little for another person. Becoming temperate means learning our limits and coming to recognize when our need for gratification begins to obscure other important values in our lives.

Fortitude: Virtue of Heroes

Unlike temperance, which helps us moderate our desires for pleasure and comfort, fortitude helps us moderate our fear and enables us to overcome our weakness and anxiety in the pursuit of good things. Often referred to as the virtue of martyrs and soldiers, who are called upon to be courageous in the face of danger, fortitude also comes in a more everyday variety that teaches us to overcome the routine fears that plague all of us as we try to live good lives.

One area in which many of us lack fortitude is in the area of commitments. While few of us deny that commitments are good things, we often fail to make them because we are afraid. Fear of criticism, fear of failure, fear of physical harm, fear of intimacy, fear of disappointment, fear of humiliation all stand in the way of commitments we make to good things. Fear is natural. But when we allow fear to limit our pursuit of the good excessively, we back ourselves into a smaller and smaller corner until at last we are afraid to go after anything we value. While it is often easier to simply give in rather than wage the fight for something we believe in, fortitude strengthens us and helps us overcome obstacles that stand in our way. Fortitude helps us see beyond our fears and take reasonable risks to secure what we know is good. Like temperance, fortitude seeks the mean: those who take foolish risks are called foolhardy; those who take no risks, even for very great goods, are called cowards.

Justice: Our Life in Community

Justice is unique because unlike the other moral virtues, it is primarily concerned with our relationships with others. This is why the term *social justice* is redundant. While temperance controls my desire, and fortitude controls my anger, justice controls my life in community.

We probably hear more explicit references to justice than to any of the other virtues. Congressional scandals, savings and loan frauds, welfare, divorce, economics, and allocation of medical care all involve questions of justice. Justice tries to assure that "each one receives according to his or her due." When we say that something is unjust, we mean that someone was deprived of something due them: often money or goods, but also truth, fidelity, or respect.

There are three kinds of justice, each dealing with certain kinds of relationships among people. Distributive justice deals with what the whole (often society) owes to the parts (individual citizens.) The most obvious example of distributive justice is in the allocation of social goods like education, police protection, firefighting resources, water and sewer services, and medical care. In each of these instances, justice determines how common goods should be distributed among many people with claims upon them. In disputed cases, judges and courts sometimes have to intervene.

Another kind of justice deals with the obligation of the parts to the whole. The payment of taxes, by which individual citizens contribute to the common good, is the most obvious example of this kind of justice. As soon as we become part of a group, we owe something to that group. Membership, as one credit-card company reminds us, may have privileges, but it also has responsibilities. Legal justice dictates how much each individual part owes to the whole.

Finally, commutative justice deals with the relationship of the parts to one another. When a young couple buy a new house, for example, they may execute a contract on that house, agreeing to pay a certain amount of money in exchange for possession of the house. Any kind of agreement like this constitutes an example of commutative justice. Taking someone to court for breach of contract or for failure to repay a loan both involve an appeal to commutative justice.

Becoming just people involves deepening our awareness that we are not merely individuals but parts of larger groups: families, villages, cities, states, nations, and now, a global community. Our membership in these groups places certain responsibilities upon us, and it guarantees us certain privileges, or rights. Justice advocates often speak about rights, but it is very important to remember that for every right there is a corresponding responsibility upon someone else. So when we speak of a "right to housing" or a "right to education" or even a "right to life," we must ask, "Upon whom does this right place a claim?" Purely abstract rights that place no specific responsibility upon anyone are empty. The "right to life" and the "right to privacy," about which we hear so much today, are what we call negative rights: unlike the right to education, which asks for something, rights to privacy and life ask to be free from something, namely, interference. But in all cases we must ask, "Upon whom does this right place a claim?" Who has the responsibility to provide education? Society? The Church? The federal government? Or who has the responsibility to leave me, or this child, free from interference? Remembering that justice always requires at least two parties—the one making the claim and the one filling it—makes seemingly intractable debates about justice issues easier to solve.

Prudence: The Heart of the Virtuous Life

We think of a "prude" as someone who is timid and afraid. Yet prudence is a strong virtue that permeates all the rest of the virtues and helps us make specific choices in concrete circumstances. It involves practical knowing: that is, it is not merely speculation, but what-is-to-be-done-in-this-case. Professionals like doctors and lawyers have to be prudent because they have to bring general rules or principles to specific cases of illness or law. Far from being just restraint, prudence also involves daring, imagination, and creativity. Among the many artistic representations of prudence, one of the most interesting is a sixteenth-century sculpture that portrays this virtue as a person with two faces. One face is that of an old man with a flowing beard, representing the wisdom, experience, and judiciousness of prudence; the other face is that of a young and lovely woman, representing prudence's flexibility, innovation, and freshness.

Prudence has several steps:

- Memory. First of all, the prudent person must learn to remember past experiences, especially those experiences similar to the one he or she is facing at the moment. The old adage "Experience is the best teacher" is appropriate here. Remembering similar situations from the past can help us do better in the present.

- Foresight. Prudence also requires that we be able to see what's ahead, especially possible obstacles or consequences to the proposed courses of action. Something might look like a good choice until we examine all of its possible ramifications; its weaknesses then become apparent.

- Imagination. Cartoonists sometimes illustrate characters who have a good idea by drawing a light bulb above their heads. The "illumination" this image suggests is crucial to good decision making. While memory and foresight are helpful in gathering knowledge, we also need to be able to put it together and discover creative solutions to difficult problems. Imagination in the moral life helps us to see possibilities that might not have occurred to us at first.[2] It helps us make connections between the good we seek and the situation with which we are faced right now. Truly prudent persons are those to whom we would turn to get insightful, imaginative solutions to difficult problems.

- Docility. The last important quality of prudence, docility does not mean submission, but openness or willingness to learn. All the memory, foresight, and imagination in the world will do us no good at all unless we are willing to be instructed or taught by it. Particularly important here is openness to the experience of others, and those who are older than we can frequently bring experience that is far beyond our own. Seeking counsel from others and allowing that counsel to shape our course of action is a key quality of prudence.

It has often been said that the moral virtues concern not the end of our lives, which is friendship and union with God, but the means to achieve that union. This friendship, which we call charity, animates the rest of the virtues; that is, it is the reason the virtues exist: to help us become closer to God through love of him. By temperance, fortitude, justice, and prudence, we are made fully human, and that makes us fully open to God's grace, uniting us with him in friendship.

Friendship is an important moral quality in itself. In many ways, the virtuous life can be said to be a life of friendship: when we achieve virtue, the various parts of our personalities (our desires, fears, needs, judgment, emotions, and so on) befriend one another and create a deep tranquillity and quality of life. That tranquillity in turn enables us to befriend others— to form friendships with others and to give birth to a just society.

For Further Reading

O'Donohoe, James. "A Return to Virtue." *Church* (Spring 1987): 48–54.

Porter, Jean. *The Recovery of Virtue: The Relevance of Aquinas for Christian Ethics.* Louisville, Ky.: Westminster/John Knox, 1990.

Waddell, Paul. *The Primacy of Love: An Introduction to the Ethics of Thomas Aquinas.* Mahwah, N.J.: Paulist, 1992.

Chapter 8

Liturgy, Friendship, and the Moral Life

We have described virtues as moral qualities or skills that are developed over the course of a lifetime. As such, they are nourished and fostered by our life of prayer and worship. The great cathedrals of Europe, for instance, frequently had stained-glass windows or sculptures portraying the virtues. They were meant to remind the faithful that the liturgy is a "school for virtue," which teaches us who we should be through music, art, and preaching.

I once heard the confession of a woman who had been away from the Church for many years. After our discussion, I suggested that she attend a special Mass the parish was celebrating that night. She asked me, "Is that my penance?" She had seen some connection between morality and liturgy, but it was the wrong one. She saw Mass as a punishment or reparation for all the years she had been away from the Church. I intended it as a healing, reconciling event, a kind of "moral lift" that would be the first step in helping her begin her life anew.

The Connection between Morality and Liturgy

We don't often associate morality with liturgy, except inasmuch as we are required by Church law to attend Mass on Sundays and certain other days. But in fact, the Church's liturgy, and especially the Eucharist, are at the root of a solid moral life. That is so because both morality and liturgy involve dialogue, remembrance, inspiration, transformation, and friendship. Let us explore each of these in turn.

Dialogue

One of my earliest memories as a Catholic is of learning the Latin responses to the Mass when I became an altar boy. When the priest said, *"Introibo ad altarem Dei"* ("I will go to the altar of God"), I learned to respond immediately, *"Ad Deum qui laetificat juventutem meum"* ("To the God who gives joy to my youth"). At the time, I didn't know what those words meant, nor did I know that I was substituting for the entire congregation. The Eucharist was a dialogue between the priest and the people, and that dialogue was meant to symbolize that the Eucharist was a participatory event. It is not a spectator sport, not something done to us or for us, but something in which we are all intimate participants.

The same is true of morality. Sometimes morality seems to be a matter of someone else imposing behavior upon us. But the moral life is a dialogue between me and God, between me and community as I shape my life. Much as the liturgical assembly sings, responds, stands, sits, and processes in unity, so we shape our moral lives with other people and in dialogue with them. In one sense it is true to say that morality is a private matter because I alone bear the responsibility for my free decisions. But in another way, morality is very much a communal event that requires the help and insight of many other people. The goal of the moral life should be to achieve some kind of harmony with those around us.

Remembering

All of our liturgical actions involve remembering. When we go to Mass, for example, we listen to the Word of the Lord, which often recalls what God has done for us. When we pray the eucharistic prayer, we remember the living and the dead, we recall the example of Mary and the saints. Most important, we remember Jesus' death and resurrection ("Christ has died...Christ is risen...Christ will come again"). This remembering is of a special kind, so powerful that it actually makes these events present here and now.

The moral life involves remembering, too. As we approach moral decisions, we must remember the moral teaching of the scriptural word, our own past experience, and the experience of the saints and others around us. In remembering, we strengthen our faith and our resolve to "do better next time."

Inspiration

Just at the middle of the eucharistic prayer, the priest says, "Lord, let your spirit come upon these gifts and make them holy...." Those words call God's life-giving Spirit not only upon the bread and wine, but upon the congregation as well. It is the Spirit whose presence makes Christ alive among us, drawing us together and binding us into one spiritual family.

The Spirit is of vital importance to the moral life, too. Often when we think of the gifts of the Holy Spirit, we think of what Christopher Kiesling referred to as the "noisy" gifts—prophecy, healing, baptism in the Spirit, slaying in the Spirit.[1] But the moral life is animated by other gifts—the "quiet" ones such as wisdom and understanding, right judgment, courage, knowledge, and reverence. Even when we have carefully trained our abilities to help us live justly, temperately, and so forth, we have never done quite enough. These gifts of the Holy Spirit are the finishing touches on our moral lives, filling them out and perfecting them. In some ways, our own efforts at morality can be compared to the work of a carpenter who "frames out" a new house. All the beams, joists, and angles are there and make a sturdy and durable base. But the gifts of the Spirit are like the work the cabinetmaker, painter, and decorator do. They finish the house off and make it livable and beautiful. Like subtle finishes on fine furniture, these gifts are not obtrusive, and we must learn to recognize them and appreciate them. As Father Kiesling said, "The spirit does not substitute for our action, but perfects it. The seeming absence of the spirit working in our lives may not be an absence at all but a presence so subtle we do not recognize it." Learning to recognize these gifts involves a special openness each time the priest invokes the Spirit upon the eucharistic offering, for that Spirit touches us as well.

Transformation

Perhaps the most dramatic similarity between liturgy and morality is transformation. No one who has ever witnessed a baptism at the Easter vigil can fail to be touched by the movement from darkness to light, or by the passing of the newly baptized through the water of salvation and into a clean white robe. These things are both signs of the transformation from death to life that takes place at baptism. Similarly, when we pray the eucharistic prayer at Mass, we hear the priest say, "This is my body...This is my blood." In so doing, he announces the transformation not only of the bread and wine, but of the whole assembly. All of us who have been baptized have been brought into the Body of Christ, and each time these words are spoken, the Spirit hovers over us and over the gifts of bread and wine, transforming them all into Christ's own body.

Unfortunately, if we focus on the eucharistic elements only, we can lose sight of this dramatic mystery. It is important for us to recall that the essence of the moral life is transformation. Just as in the Eucharist we take ordinary elements of bread and wine, in morality we take the ordinary, unformed, and incomplete elements of our lives. And just as the eucharistic action transforms that ordinary bread and wine into the body and blood of Christ, so it transforms our ordinary lives into increasingly perfect lives of virtue and grace. The wonder of the Eucharist and of the moral life is not just that it *is*, but that it *becomes*. What was once purely human and imperfect becomes, through the action of the assembly and the movement of the Spirit, a reflection of God's own self. So the eucharistic prayer should not only focus us on the altar, but lead us to feel God's transforming power within ourselves.

Friendship

As Jesus hinted when he said, "I no longer call you servants, but friends," our relationship with God is a kind of friendship. At times, this seems impossible to us because of the great distance that exists between us as humans and God who made us. Yet even after the act of creation, God has remained so close to us and so intimately involved in our lives that it is not an exaggeration for us to say that spirituality and morality are a matter of building a friendship with God.

The philosopher Aristotle said that there are three kinds of friendship. The first is useful friendship, which we cultivate because it can bring us some good. Friendships in business are sometimes of this sort. Business people become friends because their relationships can be of mutual benefit to them. They might not spend social time together, but they are friends because they have a mutual interest in their work. A second kind of friendship is one that is pleasurable; there are some people to whom we are drawn because of some quality within them that pleases us, such as wittiness or a sense of humor. We enjoy being around these people because they make us feel good, and we would consider them to be "friends" in a certain way. This kind of friendship can be unstable, however, because the relationships are based upon either some benefit to be gotten or some enjoyable quality. If the benefit or the quality disappears, the friendship may, as well.

But there is a third kind of friendship that is based neither on usefulness nor pleasure. It derives instead from the goodness that two people see in each other. This is the deepest kind of friendship, but also the most difficult to attain. Often we are attracted to people on the basis of what they can give us, or because of the pleasure we get from associating with them; but in time, we may begin to see their deeper inner goodness, and a true, lasting friendship begins to form. This is the kind of friendship we have with God. God befriends us not because we can give him anything or because we amuse him, but because he sees our deepest intrinsic goodness. We may be initially attracted to God because of what we think we can "get" (for example, salvation or holiness), but as we grow in faith we begin to realize that we love God because of his goodness, and true mutual friendship begins to develop.

Our friendship with God, as well as our true friendships with other people, develop slowly and sometimes in fits and starts. But because they are rooted in seeking the truly good in others and sharing our goodness with them, these friendships are the basis of the moral life: being moral, or truly happy, means discovering the true values of honesty, intelligence, charity, truthfulness, compassion, and strength in our friends; in return, we cultivate our own virtues so that we become more attractive to those we wish to befriend. True friends engage in a kind of covenant by which they agree to draw the very best out of each other. It is almost like two athletes who train together: they are able to see and correct each other's weaknesses, exhort each other to better performance, and share each other's victories, all the while improving themselves, too. Far from being one-sided, our relationship with God is like this, too. Though it is difficult to say that we help God "improve," God does need our love and gratitude. For example, God needs us to help realize his plan for the world. In return, God gives us his Spirit, which strengthens us and makes us holy.

Aristotle noted that friendship is at once "a state, an activity and a feeling." This reminds us that while we can be friends, and feel friendship, we must also cultivate friendship by certain kinds of activities. Friends mark their friendship by sharing meals, celebrating special events, and just spending quiet time together. Similarly, as we befriend God, we share the eucharistic meal, celebrate special moments like marriage, birth, and death, and sometimes just spend quiet time together, in prayer. Thomas Aquinas noted that "for friends to converse together is the proper condition of friendship. Our conversation with God is through contemplation." So when we pray quietly, we are really conversing with God, coming to know him better, appreciating his goodness and allowing him to appreciate ours. As we do this, we begin to see reflections of God's own goodness in those around us. We are drawn to that goodness in others not merely because it is useful or pleasurable, but because it is holy—and this becomes the basis for our friendships with others.

It would be difficult to underestimate the importance of friendship to the moral life. As Paul Waddell wrote in his marvelous book *The Primacy of Love*, "Friendships constitute our lives. Friends are those who, through their loving attention to us, sculpt us to wholeness....A good friend is someone who draws the best out of us, someone who creates us in the most promising way."[2] The importance of friends to our moral lives is obvious if we see the moral life as becoming the best possible persons we can be. Since we are often blind to much of our own goodness, friends help one another to see that goodness and make it real.

The Trinity As a Model of Friendship

In the fifteenth century, a famous artist named Rublev painted one of the world's best-known icons. It shows three identical figures seated around a table. These three persons symbolize the Trinity, and their meal symbolizes the friendship among them. But the table has an empty space, directly in front of the viewer. That empty space suggests that the Trinity invites us into their friendship to share their own life and joy. The essence of our moral and liturgical lives is the accepting of this invitation and the learning to imitate the friendship of the Trinity in our relationships with others.

For Further Reading

Aristotle. *The Ethics of Aristotle: Nichomachean Ethics.* J.A.K. Thomson, ed. New York: Penguin Books, 1955.

Waddell, Paul. *The Primacy of Love: An Introduction to the Ethics of Thomas Aquinas.* Mahwah, N.J.: Paulist, 1992. Especially chapter 4, "Charity: The Virtue of Friendship with God."

Part 3

Facing Today's Moral Dilemmas

Chapter 9

Personal Responsibility for Healthcare

With this chapter, we move from a relatively abstract discussion of the "foundations" of Christian morality to a more detailed discussion of some specific moral problems that face us and our society today. Each of the following discussions will try to provide "conscience formation" on a particular issue. These chapters will not necessarily reach conclusions (that is the role of conscience), but they will provide some of the tools necessary to reach decisions.

Medicine and medical care pose a special challenge for conscience. Medicine has probably advanced more in the last fifty years than in all of previous human history combined, and the range of medical knowledge and treatment options can seem overwhelming to even the most subtly formed conscience. Just a few of the most basic questions that medicine poses to us today are the following:

- How do I decide on treatment options for myself?
- How do I decide for others—for example, infants or the elderly—who are unable to choose and for whom I am responsible?
- How do medical specialists decide how to allocate limited medical resources such as emergency rooms, hospital beds, and specialized procedures?
- How do societies decide what portion of social resources should

be allocated to healthcare as opposed to other important social needs such as defense, education, city planning, and police protection?
- Whose responsibility is it to provide healthcare?
- Should it be equally available to all, or must it be rationed in some way? And if so, by whom?

This last question is perhaps the most difficult one that faces us in the United States today. Until now, medical care has been rationed much like any other commodity: if you have the money to pay for it (or someone to pay for you), it is available; if not, you have to do without. Although we will treat the question of healthcare rationing more fully in the next chapter, let me say here that I believe there is a "right" to healthcare much as there is a right to education, human dignity, freedom from assault, and freedom of speech. Healthcare should not be rationed by the market (that is, by economics alone) but should be distributed as equally as possible by society. I stress society, since the presumption is often that universal healthcare is the responsibility of the state or federal governments. In fact, medical knowledge and resources are a social possession for which all of us have a responsibility. It does not "belong" to the government to do with as it pleases, nor does it "belong" to individual hospitals, doctors, or medical-care personnel. They hold it in trust for the rest of us, and it is up to all of us—doctors, patients, legislators, ordinary citizens, and the Church—to help determine how to make it justly accessible to all.

Although the questions surrounding medical ethics are complex ones, there are three major areas that shed a great deal of light on most of the problems we face today.

Patient Autonomy and Informed Consent

We have already noted that conscience is the ability to know moral truth and to apply it to particular situations. In the medical arena, this translates into what we call *patient autonomy,* that is, the patient's right and obligation to make his or her own choices about medical care. *Informed consent* means simply that the patient understands his or her condition and the available treatment options, and is able to make a reasonably intelligent choice about them. Informed consent involves three things: knowledge, competence (the ability to deliberate about choices), and freedom from coercion or manipulation. This last aspect is particularly important in the case of the elderly, who are sometimes placed under pressure by their families to choose one or another course of action. Their freedom to choose can be limited in obvious ways like overmedication and physical restraint, or in more subtle ways like wistful glances or sighs from family members, excessive encouragement, or silence by physicians and other healthcare personnel.

Nor is informed consent the same thing as a consent form. Informed consent is a moral choice that may be ratified by a signature on a consent form; but it is not once-and-for-all and must be considered flexible: that is, it must often be sought and given anew, especially in long-term care or therapy, as the patient's condition and prognosis change.

Finally, while the patient himself or herself has primary responsibility for healthcare decisions, informed consent is not a solitary exercise. Because medical-care decisions are so complex, and because they often have implications for family and friends, they should really be family decisions and should flow from the patient's partnership with the physician, who often understands the patient's condition, prognosis, and options better than the patient can. While the physician usually does not decide for the patient, neither should she be a passive bystander who only provides objective information. Informed consent should be the result of a dialogue among patient, physician, and family and should always be open to revision.

Specific Treatment Decisions

After it has been determined that the necessary conditions for informed consent are present, specific treatment decisions must be made. Generally, the Catholic tradition has talked about these in terms of "ordinary and extraordinary means." Catholic theologians developed these terms centuries ago (one writer in the fifteenth century said it was acceptable to forgo a doctor's orders to eat quail eggs—which were difficult to obtain— even if they were clearly beneficial). "Ordinary" means are those we are obliged to undergo, while "extraordinary" means are those we may legitimately forgo. There is no textbook or list that describes which procedures or treatments are "ordinary," nor are they classified merely according to their cost, complexity, or availability.

Whether a treatment is ordinary or extraordinary is determined by a kind of balancing act between benefits and burdens. When faced with a decision to undergo chemotherapy for cancer, for example, we must weigh what the benefits to us will be—whether the chances are good that the treatment will improve our condition—against the burdens—the pain, expense, anxiety, and cost. And that calculation can change. While chemotherapy may be "ordinary" in the first occurrence of cancer, when cancer recurs or spreads to other parts of the body, a patient may decide that at this point the burdens of another course of chemotherapy have become too great to justify the benefits. This is where the flexibility of the terms enters in. A change in the patient's condition or state of mind may change the balance between benefit and burden, and the balance is not the same for every patient. What is "ordinary" for me, as a relatively health forty-year-old man, for example, might be extraordinary—morally nonobligatory—for an eighty-five-year-old man suffering from congestive heart failure, cancer, and diabetes.

One particularly troublesome aspect of medical choice is that of proxy judgment, which comes to play when the patient is not able to exercise informed consent for himself or herself. This may be because of noncompetence, as in the case of an infant who has never had the ability to choose, or incompetence, in the case of someone who at one time did have the ability to choose but lost it, either temporarily or permanently, because of illness. In these cases, someone else (usually the next of kin) exercises that power of choice for the patient. This may be done in one of two ways. If the patient's wishes are known, the proxy tries to duplicate those wishes as closely as possible. If the patient's wishes are not known, which is the case with infants or with young people who have never had occasion to discuss such things, the proxy makes a decision on the basis of the patient's best interests; in other words, the next of kin try to make the burdens/benefits judgment for the patient because the patient's own wishes are not known.

Congress recently enacted the Patient Self-Determination Act, which encourages all patients to provide some kind of advance directive indicating how they wish their treatment to be carried out if they are unable to decide for themselves. Advance directives are of two kinds. *Living wills*, which are implemented as soon as death threatens, specify in advance what choices the patient would want made. Living wills are limited, however, by language and terms that vary from state to state. A *durable power of attorney* becomes effective as soon as one is incapable of medical decision making, even if the patient is not in danger of death. It assigns primary responsibility for making your medical decisions to someone you trust: spouse, child, parent, or friend. Now recognized in many states, these durable powers of attorney give your delegate the power to decide for you if you are unable to do so yourself. The advantage of a durable power of attorney over a living will is that it avoids having to specify in detail all the possible medical situations that might arise. Instead, it gives general decision-making authority to one person, who can then exercise informed consent for you if you are incapacitated. But it also requires that the person delegated to make decisions for you knows and understands your wishes. Used correctly, durable powers of attorney can help keep medical decision making in the family and close to the patient, where it should be.

Forgoing and Withdrawing Life-sustaining Treatment

The most difficult question we face in medical ethics today is whether it is morally permissible to forgo or withdraw life-sustaining treatments. From what we have said above, it is clear that the Catholic tradition holds that it is permissible, provided the calculation of burdens and benefits has been made. Nor is there any significant moral difference between stopping a treatment once it has been started and not starting it at all. Sometimes we feel that once a treatment has begun, it must be continued. But in fact, the trial use of a treatment, in the hope that its benefits will be significant, may actually reveal that it is ineffective and should be discontinued.

Special interest has been focused on cases in which the "treatment" is the artificial delivery of food and water to certain classes of permanently debilitated patients. While often loosely referred to as "comatose," these patients, like Nancy Cruzan in Missouri or Claire Conroy in New Jersey, were actually classified in a different medical condition called PVS, or "permanent vegetative state." This means that because of physical trauma, lack of oxygen, or drug use, the patient's brain has been so severely damaged that it cannot recover. A small part of the brain—that part responsible for physical reflexes such as breathing, eye movement, response to pain, swallowing, and gagging—remains intact, however, and this can sometimes give the impression that the patient is conscious and responsive. A number of bishops and dioceses have issued statements on the matter, and a debate has arisen about whether it is ever permissible to remove artificial feeding from these patients. The bishops of Washington and Oregon stated the case well:

> On the one hand there are those who maintain that a permanently unconscious person who is sustained by artificially administered nutrition and hydration and is not dying from some other disease or trauma should continue to be nourished. Such nourishment is seen as part of the normal care given to any human being. Furthermore, these people would say that withdrawing artificial nutrition and hydration causes the person's death by omission and can be equivalent to euthanasia. On the other hand, there are those who insist that provision of artificial nutrition and hydration is not obligatory when the burdens clearly outweigh the benefits, and they believe this to be the case when a person has been medically diagnosed as permanently unconscious. They contend that it is an acceptable moral position to view artificially administered hydration and nutrition as a life sustaining treatment like a respirator or dialysis machine. The use of burden/benefit proportionality would indicate it is futile or burdensome or beneficial.

In April of 1992 the Committee for Pro-Life Activities of the National Conference of Catholic Bishops issued *Nutrition and Hydration: Moral and Pastoral Reflections.* In it, the bishops reviewed the state of the question and the special problems that decisions about withdrawing hydration and nutrition present. They concluded by cautiously allowing the withdrawal of hydration and nutrition in certain circumstances:

> In light of these concerns, it is our considered judgment that while the legitimate Catholic moral debate continues, decisions about these patients should be guided by a presumption in favor of medically assisted nutrition and hydration. A decision to discontinue such measures should

be made in light of a careful assessment of the burdens and benefits of nutrition and hydration for the individual patient and his or her family and community. *Such measures must not be withdrawn in order to cause death, but they may be withdrawn if they offer no reasonable hope of sustaining life or pose excessive risks or burdens.* (italics my own)

Although the 1995 encyclical *Evangelium Vitae* does not expressly address the question of withdrawing hydration and nutrition, it does affirm the right to forgo "medical procedures which no longer correspond to the real situation of the patient, either because they are by now disproportionate to any expected results or because they impose an excessive burden on the patient and his family." One may, the pope says, "refuse forms of treatment that would only secure a precarious and burdensome prolongation of life, so long as the normal care due to the sick person in similar cases is not interrupted" (#65).

Although the pope's statement is general and obviously not intended to answer every concrete case, it seems reasonable to assume that in some cases even hydration and nutrition may be seen as merely preserving this "precarious and burdensome" existence.

Those who favor allowing the removal of feeding tubes in certified cases of persistent vegetative state agree that while some benefit accrues to the patient who is maintained on a feeding tube (the patient is kept alive), the treatment is futile in view of the purpose for which we were created—to know God and love God, to be part of the human community, to grow, develop, and enjoy life. Artificially administered nutrition and hydration may maintain physical life but will never restore the person to a state enabling him or her to experience life and the grace mediated through it. In these cases, a choice to remove artificial feeding and hydration is not an act of despair or euthanasia, but an admission that the patient's illness is so severe that it makes "achievement of the purpose of life" virtually impossible, and that in an act of trust we turn that patient's life and salvation over to God.

It is important to note here that this choice to withdraw feeding and hydration, which is done regretfully, is clearly distinct from a choice of euthanasia, in which the death of the patient is directly willed. Nor is saying that one may make such a choice the same as saying that one must make such a choice. And when we do, we do so out of faith and hope rather than despair.

Does Appropriate Healthcare Change with Age?

Another difficult, yet unavoidable, question is whether the character of healthcare should change as we grow older. We have all seen statistics about the large percentage of healthcare dollars expended on patients in the last few months or even weeks of their lives. Is there not a point at which we should begin asking, "How much healthcare is too much?" Advance directives and durable powers of attorney help, but as Christians we need to begin reshaping our overall spiritual presuppositions about life. Sometimes, grasping life too tightly can be a spiritual disease.

Daniel Callahan, a noted healthcare ethicist, has proposed that we begin to think in terms of "biographical age." Is there a point, he has asked, when our natural life is pretty much drawing to a close, even though we may be in relatively good health? Is there a point when our attitude should shift away from life-prolonging technology and toward the gracious acceptance of death? He has written:

> There are large and growing numbers of elderly who are not imminently dying, but who are feeble and declining, for whom curative medicine has little to offer....For many, old age is a reason in itself to think about medical care in a different way, whether in forgoing its lifesaving powers when death is clearly imminent, or in forgoing its use even when death may be distant but life has become a blight rather than a blessing.[1]

He cites the heavy bias of the Medicare program toward saving and extending life and away from primary care, comfort, and palliation. In some cases, the bias toward high-technology lifesaving measures is so strong that it's only with difficulty that one can enforce choices for comfort and pain relief only. Norman Paradis has written of such a case in the treatment of his own father:

> When I finally got my father's physicians on the phone, I insisted that he be cared for only by internists who had no incentive to do anything but make him comfortable. Yet my father had been in the hospital two weeks and had spent most of that time receiving "billable" high tech therapy that could not possibly cure him or relieve his pain. We had to forbid them to do anything that was not directly related to relieving his pain.[2]

Callahan believes such cases could be avoided if we allow the elderly to choose their own balance between high-technology curative medicine and low-technology care and social support.

The spiritual dimension of such choices is related to asceticism. Philip Keane, in his book, *Health Care Reform: A Catholic Perspective*, has written about the importance of cultivating asceticism as we make our healthcare choices:

> When talking about asceticism we need to be careful not to glorify suffering so that we end up embracing some sort of spiritual masochism. But the ascetic tradition [does] tell us that we need to grasp life lightly, that we sometimes need to be willing to let go of our own personal interests and priorities for the sake of higher values and for the sake of other people....[3]

It is important that we carefully differentiate between the consideration of age as a factor in deciding what kind of care is appropriate, and the arguments in support of proposals for euthanasia or assisted suicide. Allowing people to choose the way in which their final illnesses will be managed is ethically quite distinct from neglecting them, killing them, or helping them kill themselves.

A discussion this short runs the risk of oversimplifying the complexity of medical ethical decisions. But the areas we have discussed provide at least the very basic outlines of how to approach such questions. Enhancing patient knowledge and freedom, consulting with family and knowledgeable experts, and remembering that we were not created just to live out our physical lives, but to "know God, love God, and be with God forever in heaven" are all important ingredients in making good choices in medical care.

For Further Reading

DeBlois, Jean, Mary McGrath, and Kevin O'Rourke. *Advance Directives for Future Health Care Decisions: A Christian Perspective.* St. Louis: Virginia Publishing Co. (232 N. Kingshighway, #205, 63108), 1991. This small booklet provides both the Christian rationale for advance directives and the appropriate legal format.

DeBlois, Jean, Patrick Norris, and Kevin O'Rourke. *A Primer for Health Care Ethics: Essays for a Pluralistic Society.* Washington, D.C.: Georgetown University Press, 1994.

Gula, Richard M. *Euthanasia: Moral and Pastoral Perspectives.* Mahwah, N.J.: Paulist, 1994.

McCarthy, Jeremiah J., and Judith Caron. *Medical Ethics: A Catholic Guide to Health Care Decisions.* Liguori, Mo.: Liguori, 1990.

McCormick, Richard A. *Health and Medicine in the Catholic Tradition.* New York: Crossroad, 1984.

O'Rourke, Kevin, and Philip Boyle. *Medical Ethics: Sources of Catholic Teachings.* Washington, D.C.: Georgetown University Press, 1993.

Pope John Paul II. *Evangelium Vitae (The Gospel of Life).* New York: Times Books, 1995, especially nos. 64–67 on euthanasia and suicide.

Chapter 10

Social Responsibility
for Healthcare Reform

In addition to being a personal responsibility, healthcare is also a social question. The allocation of healthcare has been hotly debated in recent years. What are the possible options for reorganizing healthcare?

Options for the Future

The media recently carried a story about a promising young professional athlete who had developed symptoms of heart problems. He consulted a team of eleven cardiac specialists who advised him that it would be dangerous for him to continue playing sports. Unwilling to admit the loss of his career, he consulted other doctors until he found one who told him that his condition was not so serious as first thought and that he could consider continuing his career if he had a cardiologist and cardiac equipment present at every game. None of the commentators or news stories questioned the legitimacy of having a cardiologist present for the benefit of one patient who was deliberately placing his health at risk, and no one noted the irony of this extravagant medical care in a country where at least 14 percent of the population—somewhere between 35 and 40 million people—have no healthcare insurance at all, and where many others have only sporadic access to healthcare.

The United States has the most sophisticated healthcare resources in the world, and most Americans say they are satisfied with the healthcare they receive. Yet despite the fact that we spend more than $700 billion per year on healthcare ($2 billion per day, or nearly $10 per day for every man, woman, and child in the land), many of us have inadequate care. Nearly everyone acknowledges today that the way we allocate healthcare must undergo serious reform, but there is no agreement on what a reformed system should look like. Let us quickly review the current state of healthcare delivery and the proposals for reform.

The Current State of Healthcare

Healthcare coverage in this country cannot be called a "system." It is a patchwork of various kinds of programs, federal and private, that provide some healthcare to some people, some of the time. It is filled with gaps and duplications, and it is very expensive. What coverage we have could be characterized as "three-sided," based on Medicare, Medicaid, and a variety of privately funded programs.

Medicare was inaugurated in the 1960s as a way of providing basic healthcare to those over age sixty-five. It has functioned reasonably well, but it has grown with the cost and complexity of healthcare itself, and today it threatens to overwhelm the premiums paid by working and retired persons. There are gaps in its coverage that must be filled by private "supplemental" insurance or by other government entitlement programs. Today it provides coverage for about 13 percent of the population, or about 35 million people.

Medicaid was mandated by the government as a means of providing healthcare to the poor and disabled, and it is run by the various states. This causes difficulties when particular states experience financial problems that prevent them from meeting all the coverage requirements established by the government. In addition, Medicare patients who do not have supplemental insurance must often fall back on Medicaid to cover things such as nursing-home care when they are not reimbursed by Medicare. In 1990, about 10 percent of the population, or 25 million people, were covered by Medicaid.

Private insurance is the largest category of healthcare coverage and is held by about 74 percent of the population. Of this group, more than half are covered by employer-provided health plans, and about 13 percent are covered by privately purchased, nongroup insurance. These plans include traditional insurance plans, which grant patients complete freedom to choose physicians and healthcare facilities, as well as health maintenance organizations (HMOs) and preferred provider organizations (PPOs), which place some restrictions on which doctors you may see or what hospitals or clinics you may use. Insurance tends to provide reimbursement on a "fee for services" basis and usually requires that the patient pay some expenses out of pocket in the form of a deductible. HMOs and PPOs usually provide coverage on a "capitation" basis, meaning that the patient or employer pays a single, "per capita" charge for coverage and receives no itemized bills.

Although those who have one of the above forms of coverage usually have adequate healthcare, they must live with the fear of losing it if they change or lose their jobs. In addition, these three means of coverage leave 10–15 percent of the population permanently without insurance.

Proposals for Reform

The rapidly rising costs of healthcare and the gaps in coverage I have described above have led to dozens of proposals by legislators, state and federal governments, and private associations for reforming healthcare to provide more complete, reliable, and efficient coverage. Although they vary widely, these proposals can be grouped into three broad categories: "fixing" the present three-part system; expanding "managed competition" and moving toward universal coverage; adopting a single-payer system. We will examine each of these, then explore the values that underpin Catholic social teaching and the ways in which they might guide reform efforts.

Fixing the Present System

The most conservative approach would be to expand the current, three-part system of healthcare by retaining Medicare and Medicaid much as they currently exist and increasing the availability of private health insurance by means of tax credits that would allow families below a certain income level to buy private insurance. President Bush offered such a proposal toward the end of his term. The advantage of these measures is that they protect the insurance industry and favor free-market competition over government control. Their weakness lies in the fact that they try to build on a haphazard and poorly coordinated network of services that nearly everyone agrees is wasteful and not distributed equally; the elderly poor, for example, are paying a larger and larger portion of their own medical costs, straining their meager incomes to the limit. The other major problem with proposals that would "fix" the present system is that they let private healthcare and insurance concerns dictate the future shape of healthcare with virtually no government leadership. I will explain later why such leadership is crucial.

Move to "Managed Competition"

The types of proposals that appear to have the most support in 1995 are those that retain elements of competition, which Americans believe makes everything better, while trying to "manage" it in a constructive way. This would be accomplished by the establishment of a minimum-standard healthcare package that would then be offered by a variety of competing companies and purchased by employers. Competition would be "managed" by standardizing policy benefits and setting an annual cap on healthcare spending. The weakness of these proposals is that they place a heavy burden on employers, who would either have to "play" by purchasing health insurance or health coverage through HMOs or PPOs or their own programs, or "pay" a special tax that would provide coverage for their employees.

President Clinton offered proposals along these lines in 1993, specifying a basic package of healthcare benefits, assuring free choice of doctors, initiating tighter regulation of insurance coverage and drug prices, and reducing red tape.

Another variation would take monies currently spent on Medicare, Medicaid, and private insurance and distribute them to families as a kind of "medical savings account." Families would pay their initial medical expenses out of this account; expenses in excess of the amount in the account would be paid for by insurance purchased by employers. Employees who have a good year with no medical problems could keep the money. Proponents argue that this plan would enable employers to fund the savings accounts and buy insurance for less than they are currently paying for insurance alone. It would save money because patients would have an incentive to shop around and use their healthcare dollars frugally, something the present system of reimbursement does not provide.

The "Single-Payer" System

The "single-payer" system is the third and most innovative of the three general categories of reform plans. This plan would eliminate Medicare, Medicaid, and private insurance and replace all three of them with a single payer, probably a federal or state agency. Such proposals for universal coverage were proposed as early as 1942, but they have never been able to gain sufficient public support for enactment.

Although specific proposals vary, most of them would create a federal healthcare board to predetermine types of coverage and levels of reimbursement. Actual payment would be made by individual states from revenues currently expended on Medicare, Medicaid, and private insurance. States could process claims themselves or contract with insurance companies to do that for them. Some additional taxation may be required as well, but proponents say this could be offset by the elimination of insurance premiums. Unlike "socialized medicine" (in which healthcare facilities are owned by the government and medical personnel are government employees, as is the case in England), a single-payer system would retain private hospitals and physicians much as we have now. The significant difference is that the bureaucracy and paperwork now required by insurance reimbursement would be replaced by automatic payments at previously determined levels. Physicians or hospitals who wish to charge more than the fees set by the health board could do so, but patients would be required to pay those additional charges "out of pocket." Coverage would be universal, would not depend on employment, and would not place a disproportionate burden on employers.

The present three-sided approach to healthcare coverage developed piecemeal over the last thirty years or so. It began to emerge in an era before antibiotics, chemotherapy, brain surgery, and advanced life-support systems. It was never meant to accommodate bone-marrow transplants, gene splicing, or medications costing thousands of dollars per dose. The rise of the average life expectancy alone has placed tremendous pressure on Medicare, which pays 30 percent of its claims for care in the last twelve months of life. While these advances have been a great blessing to us, they are forcing us to make very difficult decisions about how to divide our national resources among various basic goods such as education, defense, and healthcare. But even more difficult are the decisions about how to allocate our healthcare dollars among competing needs for childhood care, acute care, and long-term care for the elderly.

Most of the proposals we have examined try in some measure to realize the "right to healthcare." Because healthcare is a basic human need, there is a "right" to it. But in order for a right to mean anything, it must be met by a corresponding obligation, as we saw in chapter 7.

In the case of healthcare, our "right" is based on the fact that healthcare is something we all need, but which none of us can provide on our own. This creates a network of interdependence among us and calls for a kind of cooperation that is rooted in the virtue of justice.

The Catholic Tradition of Justice

Given the range of possibilities of healthcare reform, how do we choose which is best? The Catholic tradition does not provide a detailed solution, but it does provide several very important principles.

Sacramentality and the Uniqueness of Healthcare

Because we are created "in the image of God," and because Christ became incarnate in a human body, our bodies are sacraments or "temples of the Holy Spirit." This means that they actually reveal God to us and to others, and that we experience grace through our bodies rather than in spite of them. Our bodies are not just shells that hold our spirits but are mysterious realizations of the power and love of God. Serious illness can provide us with an experience of the redemptive power of suffering. But it also impedes our work, our relationships, and our prayer. It can cause serious depression and make us lose interest in everything we hold dear.

This makes healthcare, which preserves and heals the human body, unlike any other kind of human service.

Yet despite the importance of our bodies and the care that keeps them healthy, physical life is not an absolute value nor an end in itself. Those of us who learned from the Baltimore Catechism remember that it taught us that God created us to "know him, love him and serve him in this world, and be with him forever in heaven," and it is that final union with God that is our real goal in life. So while we should take every reasonable step to assure our good health so that we are able to experience the sacramentality of life fully, there are times when Christians must face the fact of mortality and gracefully accept the reality of terminal illness or death. This is why it is inappropriate for Christians to want "everything possible" in healthcare. There are times when what is possible is not reasonable, given the unlikelihood of success. Healthcare should enhance life, but it should not deny the reality of death. When healthcare becomes too aggressive, it not only does not help us spiritually, it can actually be an obstacle to our hope in the Resurrection.

Justice and the Right to Healthcare

Many people fear that healthcare reform is primarily a matter of raising taxes and putting the government into the business of providing healthcare. But the reality is much more complicated than that. Healthcare reform is not just a matter of more or less government involvement, but of achieving justice. Because it is such a fundamental human good, healthcare is the responsibility of society—doctors, patients, taxpayers, politicians, religious leaders cooperating together in the achievement of the common good. Society may *use* government as a means to providing healthcare, but the responsibility for providing these basic goods falls squarely on us. We cannot abdicate that responsibility to government, but neither can we ignore the role of government in helping to bring this reality about.

As discussed in chapter 7, justice is the virtue that assures "each receives his or her due." As a virtue, it is an acquired moral vision and a corresponding tendency to act or choose in a certain way. The just person (or society) will habitually distribute both goods and responsibilities equitably. This means, on the one hand, that healthcare benefits should be allocated according to need and according to what is best for all of us together. As Philip Keane has noted, Americans are possessed of a pervasive individualism that often makes it hard for us to choose in the best long-range interest of the community. This is particularly evident when we base our politics and our vote on the value of low taxes alone. Because politics today is so complicated, many voters have fixated on the slogan "no new taxes" as though that policy would solve all our problems. In the wake of so-called "tax revolts," public funding for education, healthcare, public safety, and public services like transportation have been cut to the bone and are being replaced by private services that only those of means can afford.

No one disputes that low taxes are a good thing. Our tradition clearly teaches that we should always allow for the greatest freedom possible, and that extends even to the freedom to earn and spend as we like. But our tradition also tells us that as members of a society, we are part of a living social organism and have a responsibility to those around us, without whose cooperation we cannot eat, be educated, or secure healthcare. Even as we keep taxes low, we must be realistic about the costs of keeping this social organism healthy and remember that we cannot simply opt for the benefits of society without incurring an obligation. I might speak of "my right to healthcare," but in the end it has to be *our* right to healthcare, for if even one of us is sick, all of us are diminished. When we enter into the healthcare-reform debate, we need to set aside our own private interests and ask, "What kind of healthcare do *we* need?" rather than "What kind of healthcare do *I* need?"

Who Pays the Bills?

One of the most contentious issues in healthcare reform is "Who is going to pay for it?" This, too, concerns justice, since the costs as well as the goods of healthcare have to be justly distributed. It should be obvious from our brief overview of the current situation that costs are very unequally distributed. Some people with private health insurance pay thousands of dollars per year for their care, while others pay little or nothing. Justice is proportional. It does not assign benefit or responsibility in equal measure but according to need and resources. Thus the Catholic tradition clearly teaches that those with the greatest need should come first, and those with the greatest resources should contribute first. The basic principle should be that we "receive according to our need and pay according to our ability." This is not just a handout but an investment in the health of the community of which we are integral parts.

Since healthcare is something we all need, taxation must be borne as equally as possible by all of us. Many of the current proposals for healthcare reform call for increased taxes on cigarettes and liquor. Although these items may in some ways be considered nonessentials or luxuries, it would not be fair to make smokers or drinkers bear a disproportionate burden for the healthcare of the entire population. The funding for such a broadly based social good should be spread across the entire population.

Setting Priorities

After the fear of taxes, the greatest obstacle to serious healthcare reform is the fear of rationing. Though the term is rarely defined clearly, to many people it suggests long waits for essential treatments or arbitrary denials of required treatments. Our medical resources are vast, and those who have access to medical care have become accustomed to have as much as they want when they want it.

The experiences of other countries, such as Canada, suggest that the amount that we spend on healthcare now should enable us to provide universal access with very few waits and restrictions on only the most exotic and marginally effective treatments. This is not rationing but a sensible establishment of priorities.

Justice is not an exact science, but it surely dictates that we begin with what is best for the greatest number of us most of the time. That means setting up a system in which everyone has immediate access to basic, preventative, and emergency care. That will leave plenty of resources to provide for more advanced and less clearly effective treatments like heart surgery, cancer therapy, and organ transplants. Setting priorities also means carefully evaluating treatments "at the edges of life." Would any of us, for example, opt to provide unlimited therapies for seriously ill newborns who have a very slim chance of survival or for the terminally ill who have no reasonable chance of cure if doing so means sacrificing preventive prenatal care, childhood vaccinations, or emergency services for trauma victims? None of us wants such choices to be arbitrary, but the overall health of the community requires that we establish priorities that serve all of us most effectively in the long run. It also requires that we admit the limits of our medical ability, accept the grace of death, and avoid expensive and futile overtreatment.

Altruism and Efficiency in Healthcare

Throughout most of history, healthcare has been seen as an altruistic, other-directed activity, undertaken for its own rewards. Recently, we have begun to see it as just another business, and sometimes as a business from which disinterested investors can make a profit. Because healthcare is such a basic and personal need, we must honestly ask ourselves whether it is compatible with profit-making insurance companies and healthcare facilities.

Greater efficiency should also be the goal of any healthcare reform. This means keeping paperwork and bureaucracy at a minimum. Although competition invigorates business, in healthcare it has often led to needless duplication of equipment and services and aggressive advertising for patients. This results in an unacceptable and inefficient diversion of dollars from direct healthcare and from the compensation of healthcare personnel and reduces the effectiveness of healthcare delivery.

Healthcare Reform and Catholic Identity

Because Catholic institutions have been so influential in shaping today's healthcare, we have a strong interest in seeing that certain of our values are not overlooked. One of the most important is what is often referred to as the sanctity of life, a concept that concerns reproduction, abortion, and care of the seriously ill.

Almost everyone knows the substance of Catholic teaching on abortion and artificial contraception. A teaching on the withdrawal or withholding of life-sustaining treatment for the seriously ill is still developing, but many Catholics are concerned that healthcare reforms that give greater control to government will weaken our long-held respect for life. This is a legitimate concern, and we have every right to bring it to bear on the debate about healthcare reform.

As we do so, however, we must remember that our views on these matters do not stem primarily from our religious faith. That is, we do not believe abortion, sterilization, and euthanasia are wrong only because revelation tells us so, but because we see these acts as generally harmful to us as human persons, as discussed in chapter 5. In a sense, we can say that Catholics speak two moral languages: a religious, or biblical, language that says, "This act is wrong because it is an affront to the image of God within me"; and a language of reason or philosophy by which we can say, "This act is wrong because it is inhuman, and it violates what it means to be a person."

Even those who do not share our religious faith can speak that second language with us and dialogue about how the dignity of the human person might be safeguarded. This dialogue is sometimes a messy, exasperating process. No rational person wants to destroy human dignity, but there can be legitimate disagreements over the best ways to protect it. Sometimes our involvement in this dialogue will require compromise as other persons of goodwill disagree with us about the best way in which to promote human dignity. Since healthcare is a central part of the common good, we are bound to enter into the dialogue and to argue our view of human good as cogently and sincerely as we can. In the interest of securing the best overall healthcare for all of us, we may have to settle for less than 100 percent of our understanding of how best to protect that dignity.

In areas where healthcare services are scarce, Catholic healthcare facilities may have to enter into joint ventures with other institutions that provide abortions or other procedures we find morally objectionable. While such cooperation involves risks and must be undertaken prudently, in some cases it may be the only way of ensuring any Catholic presence at all, or of assuring basic healthcare for children and the elderly. The norms for such ventures are found in the U.S. bishops' *Ethical and Religious Directives for Catholic Health Care Services* (Washington, D.C.: 1994):

> New partnerships can be viewed as opportunities for Catholic health care institutions and services to witness to their religious and ethical

commitments and so influence the healing profession. For example, new partnerships can help to implement the church's social teaching....realign the local delivery system in order to provide a continuum of health care to the community...witness to a responsible stewardship of limited health resources [or] provide to poor and vulnerable persons a more equitable access to basic care.

On the other hand, new partnerships can pose serious challenges to the viability of the identity of Catholic health care....The risk of scandal cannot be underestimated when partnerships are not built upon common values and moral principles (#66).

The Catholic tradition in healthcare has a long and venerable history that stresses equal access to the goods of healthcare and proportional responsibility for providing it. It realizes that the means of healthcare, including medical education and training, do not belong to any one individual but are the result of the cooperation of many generations of patients, physicians, nurses, and researchers whose accumulated efforts have created the marvelous resources we have today. Above all, our tradition stresses that healthcare affirms human dignity and sacramentality in a way few other human undertakings can. It calls us to commit ourselves to the restructuring of our current, inadequate means of healthcare delivery and to support proposals that provide the most comprehensive and efficient care with the broadest possible funding base.

Chapter 11

Morality and Public Life: Political Choices in a Diverse Society

A quick glance at the history books shows that for most of the last two thousand years, religious and civil authority were one and the same. Popes crowned emperors and even had armies that waged fierce battles against kings and princes. There was no such thing as a distinctively civil government that did not have its roots in a divine order presided over by bishops, priests, and monks.

All that changed dramatically at the end of the eighteenth century. Suddenly, a half-century of revolutions rudely challenged the Church's political prerogatives, displacing religious authority with a new kind of civil authority that had no direct links to the Church and that functioned by virtue of reason rather than revelation or religion. All over Europe, royal families were put to death, churches and monasteries were seized by the government or destroyed, and many priests and religious were forced into exile. At about the same time, the thirteen original colonies of the United States were coalescing into a nation—and they did so in a radically new way. The framers of the American Constitution declared that the state was to establish no religion as "official." All would be free to practice their religious beliefs as they wished. The American experiment sundered the connection between religious and civil authority once and for all and set the Church entirely on its own.

In many ways, this was a great blessing to the Church. Now forced to fend for itself and unable to rely upon state support, it would grow quickly and become strong and self-sufficient. The United States remained deeply religious, and there were many bitter disputes about just how religion was to find a home in an officially nonreligious country. Today, this tension finds expression in disputes about various schemes for public support of private schools, debates about whether school prayer should be tolerated or even sponsored by the government, and pressure to present biblical accounts of creation on an equal footing with evolutionary theories. Although few Catholics have difficulty reconciling the scientific theory of evolution with Biblical accounts of creation, there are many other areas in which public laws and policies seem to compromise our moral beliefs. Federal or state laws on abortion, AIDS information, civil rights for homosexuals, religious education in public schools, and a host of other issues pose serious dilemmas for Catholics. How can we support laws that violate our basic moral convictions? Shouldn't the laws we enact reflect the moral truths we know to be true? Sometimes it seems as though the only two alternatives available to us are withdrawal from a sinful society or imposition of our convictions on a nation. A number of important distinctions might help clarify this thorny question.

Morality and Religion

The first thing we need to remember as we enter these debates is that morality and religion are not necessarily the same thing. There are many moral traditions, including the Roman Catholic one, that begin with a reasoned understanding of the human person rather than with revelation or Scripture. This view of the person, enlightened and clarified by our faith, becomes the basis for deciding what is moral and what is not. Most of the difficult social questions we face today—abortion, civil rights, medical ethics—are not and cannot be decided purely on the basis of our religious faith. In many instances the Bible has nothing at all to say on these topics, so we are left to our intelligence and reason to discover answers. While we sometimes equate "moral" with "religious," in fact there is a more basic moral code, one that we might call "common human morality," that all reasonable people can seek and understand. In a pluralistic society, it is this common moral base, and not the imposition of religious views, that we must seek.

In the abortion debate, for example, opponents of abortion rightly argue from a pro-life stance. Yet their arguments often appeal to the words of Scripture and make it seem as though only religious believers can understand these arguments. Pro-choice activists reject these arguments as "merely religious" and say that they have no place in a society in which there is no established religion. "I do not share your religious faith," they say, "therefore, your arguments in favor of the God-given sanctity of life are not convincing to me." Abortion is surely a moral issue, but it is not necessarily a religious issue. Anybody who understands what human life is—and one does not need religious faith to do that—can understand why abortion might be wrong. Political candidates who state that they are opposed to abortion on the basis of their religious belief but do not want to impose that belief on others are placing abortion in a strictly religious category—and that makes it easy to reject arguments against abortion. In a pluralistic society our task is not to impose our views on others but to try to convince others of our deeply held convictions by cogent, well-reasoned arguments.

Morality and Public Policy

The second important distinction is between morality and public policy. Morality (and this includes both religious morality and "common sense" morality) is geared to personal perfection. It is internal, intentional, and deeply personal. Like charm or character or honesty, it cannot be forced upon someone but must flow from within. In this sense, it is true to say that "morality cannot be legislated"—it can only be freely assumed by people who have chosen it because of its evident beauty.

Public policy or civil law, on the other hand, has a much more modest goal. Unlike morality, which aims at the inner perfection of persons, laws and public policies aim only at public order. Pope John Paul II's 1995 encyclical *Evangelium Vitae* (#71) affirms this distinction. For this reason, laws that regulate drinking, banking, or the sale of guns do not make people moral but create the relatively harmonious and peaceful environment in which we are able to pursue morality. Few of us, for example, would be able to cultivate the virtues of truth, prudence, temperance, or patience if we lived in a society that was torn by strife and insurrection.

Public policy tries to achieve the minimum necessary for all of us to live together in peace. It tries to protect us from danger, provide basic goods like housing, education, medical care, and employment, and regulate the distribution of commodities like electricity, fuel, and food. These things are all vitally necessary and enable us to seek morality, but they are not the same thing as morality.

The truth of this distinction is evident if we think for a moment about things that are *moral but not legal:* it may not be a sin to exceed the speed limit, drink alcohol after 2:00 A.M., park in a no-parking zone, or refuse to report for military duty, but each of these are usually seen as violations of the law and will be punished as such. There are also things that are *legal but not moral:* sex with someone other than your spouse, "bending" laws to limit employee wages, drinking to excess, lust, and so forth. And of course, there are things that may be both illegal and immoral: cheating, bribery, lying, killing. The important thing to note here is that there is not a perfect correspondence between civil laws, which govern our life together and create a harmonious social context, and morality, which governs our personal lives and makes us good persons. The two are not unrelated, but they are not exactly the same either. Confusing them often results in disaster, as did the unfortunate attempt to prohibit the consumption of alcohol in this country in the 1920s. Not only did prohibition not create a nation of temperate men and women, it created widespread disregard for the law and may well have given birth to organized crime, which plagues us to this day. Laws that try to enforce morality or that do not have adequate support from the community on which they are imposed are bad laws and are doomed to failure.

The abortion issue is one of those cases today in which morality and public policy do not always intersect. While many people feel that abortion is immoral because it is murder, many others feel just as strongly that it is not murder and should be placed in another category. The problem is that there is a fundamental disagreement about what kind of act abortion is. Is it a noble act of free choice or the deliberate taking of human life? Until now, at least, this fundamental disagreement has made consensus on abortion impossible.

Although we may be convinced that the embryo is a person from the moment of conception and that abortion is, therefore, seriously immoral, many other people of goodwill would disagree with us. This does not mean that we should water down our own convictions. But we must remember that good law—which is always oriented to public order—must be feasible: that is, it must have the support of a significant portion of the populace before it can be enacted. While abortion may indeed be immoral, it is not clear that sufficient public consensus exists today to eliminate abortion by legislation. Consequently, we will have to find other strategies to reduce or eliminate abortions. Doing so does not mean we are "soft on abortion" but that we are realistic about what legislation can and cannot accomplish. Simply declaring that human life exists at a certain point or making abortion illegal on that basis will not stop abortion unless a significant proportion of the population agrees with those presuppositions.

Politics and *The Gospel of Life*

In his 1995 encyclical *The Gospel of Life (Evangelium Vitae)*, Pope John Paul II offers a detailed analysis of the cultural trends that threaten life. The issues he treats—abortion, embryo experimentation, euthanasia, suicide, and capital punishment—are all moral issues, but they have important implications for civil law as well. This makes the encyclical of interest to legislators and citizens alike.

The pope begins with the biblical story of Cain, who in the fourth chapter of Genesis killed his brother Abel out of jealousy. When God asked Cain what he had done, Cain asked, "Am I my brother's keeper?" Just as Cain "does not wish to think about his brother and refuses to accept the responsibility which every person has towards others," so in our own society this trend is manifest in an emerging "culture of death," in which "broad sectors of public opinion justify certain crimes against life in the name of rights of individual freedom, and on this basis they claim not only exemption from punishment but even authorization by the state…" (#4). The pope sees symptoms of this disregard for life in the lack of solidarity with "society's weakest members—such as the elderly, the infirm, immigrants, children—and the indifference frequently found in relations between the world's peoples even when basic values such as survival, freedom and peace are involved" (#8).

The pope lists several factors that have brought this cultural situation about: a profound crisis of culture, which generates skepticism in relation to the very foundations of knowledge and ethics, and which makes it increasingly difficult to grasp clearly the meaning of what a person is. Then there are all kinds of existential and interpersonal difficulties, made worse by the complexity of a society in which individuals, couples, and families are often left alone with their problems. Finally, there are situations of acute poverty, anxiety, or frustration, in which "the struggle to make ends meet, the presence of unbearable pain, or instances of violence, especially against women, make the choice to defend and promote life so demanding as sometimes to reach the point of heroism" (#11).

The roots of this problem lie in an extreme subjectivity, which "recognizes as a subject of rights only the person who enjoys full or at least incipient autonomy and who emerges from a state of total dependence on others." This in turn heightens individual freedom so much that any notion of life in society is distorted, and there is no place for "solidarity, openness to others and service of them...." Eventually, everyone is considered an enemy from whom one has to defend oneself. "Society becomes a mass of individuals placed side by side, but without any mutual bonds" (#19, 20).

The pope suggests that commitment to the gospel of life, which "includes everything that human experience and reason tell us about the value of human life, accepting it, purifying it, exalting it and bringing it to fulfillment" (#30), will remedy this sad trend. He specifically addresses a number of human-life issues that are currently under consideration by legislative bodies around the world.

Capital Punishment (#55–56)

Although he stresses the inviolability of the command "Do not kill," the pope admits that there are some cases, analogous to self-defense, in which "the right to protect one's own life and the duty not to harm someone else's life are difficult to reconcile in practice." While it is never legitimate to take the life of an innocent person, the pope says that because governments have a right and duty to protect the lives of their citizens, there may be cases in which a criminal poses such a grave threat to a society that only taking his or her life will provide safety to other citizens. Punishments for crimes ought to "fulfil [*sic*] the purpose of defending public order and ensuring people's safety, while at the same time offering the offender an incentive and help to change his or her behavior and be rehabilitated." He allows that, in very rare circumstances, execution may be necessary, but only "when it would not be possible otherwise to defend society. Today however…such cases are very rare, if not practically non-existent."

The pope's view is dependent on seeing society as a whole, as a kind of organism or body that sometimes has diseased or dysfunctional parts that must be removed for the good of the whole. Viewed from this perspective, the death penalty should not be seen as a retribution but as a regrettable necessity, invoked only when the criminal poses a direct threat to society. Except in emergencies or wartime, it is difficult to imagine circumstances in which execution is the only possible way of eliminating the threat that a criminal poses to public safety.

Abortion and Embryonic Experimentation (#58–63)

The most difficult moral questions we face today revolve around the rights of unborn children. As I have already pointed out, the problem is rooted in controversy about the status of the embryo. Many members of our society will not acknowledge the full personhood of the embryo and will not grant it the protection of the law.

The pope acknowledges the centuries-long controversy about the exact moment at which the embryo is "ensouled" and becomes a human person. He admits that there is no scientific way to demonstrate when this occurs but says that if the existence of a human person is probable, it should be protected:

> Even if the presence of a spiritual soul cannot be ascertained by empirical data, the results themselves of scientific research on the human embryo provide "a valuable indication for discerning by the use of reason a personal presence at the moment of the first appearance of a human life: how could a human individual not be a human person?"…the mere probability that a human person is involved would suffice to justify an

absolutely clear prohibition of any intervention aimed at killing a human embryo (#60).

In cases like this in which there may be some doubt, it is useful to recall an example that moral theologians used for centuries. They cited the case of a hunter in the woods who saw movement among the trees. A glimpse was not enough to determine whether the movement was caused by a person or a deer. Should the hunter go ahead and shoot anyway, hoping to hit a deer? Moral theologians always held that in such cases, in which there was even a small possibility that a person had caused the movement, the prudent hunter would refrain from firing. The pope's argument about abortion is similar. Even if the biological or genetic "glimpse" we have of the embryo cannot prove definitively that the embryo is ensouled from the moment of conception, it is certainly possible, and even probable, that it is. Rather than risk the deliberate killing of an innocent child, we should rule out abortion in every case.

The same argument applies to embryonic research that is not directed to healing or that involves disproportionate risks or side effects to the embryo. Just as we would not use adults as involuntary objects of experimentation (the horrible experiments of Nazi doctors on living subjects comes to mind), so, too, if embryos are, or even might be, full persons, we must not objectify them by making them "matter" for experiments that are of no benefit to them.

An even more drastic case involves deliberately bringing an embryo into existence for the express purpose of experimentation or therapy for another person. A television hospital drama once related the case of a man who was suffering from rapidly advancing Parkinson's disease, which causes progressive damage to the nervous system. Because there is some evidence that fetal brain tissue may halt or reverse the damage caused by the disease, he and his wife agreed to get pregnant in order to create an embryo whose brain tissue could then be harvested and used therapeutically to halt the progress of his disease. Their plans were a clear violation of the dignity of that embryo, as the pope says clearly when he speaks of procedures that exploit living human embryos and fetuses—sometimes specifically "produced" for this purpose by *in vitro* fertilization—either to be used as "biological material" or as *providers of organs or tissue for transplants* in the treatment of certain diseases. The killing of innocent human creatures, even if carried out to help others, constitutes an absolutely unacceptable act (#63).

Suicide and Euthanasia (#64–67)

The third threat that the pope sees to the gospel of life is a tendency in our prosperous and efficient societies to see the "growing number of elderly and disabled people as intolerable and burdensome" (#64). This may lead us to consider euthanasia, which by omission or commission involves an intention to "take control of death and bring it about before its time." The pope carefully distinguishes these intentional acts of killing from choices to forgo futile or aggressive treatments that offer little hope to the patient. Even painkillers that may hasten death are permissible as long as the intent is only to relieve pain and is in no way to cause the patient's death. Patients may choose, of course, to accept some pain to "share consciously in the Lord's Passion," but the pope considers such a choice heroic and not the duty of everyone. Repeating the teaching of Pope Pius XII, Pope John Paul II notes that the use of painkillers is licit, even if they shorten life, as long as "death is not willed or sought, even though for reasonable motives one runs the risk of it" (65).

The culture of death can also make suicide seem like an honorable choice, especially in old age or in the face of serious, progressive illness. But *Evangelium Vitae* insists that suicide remains a "grave evil" that "involves the rejection of love of self and the renunciation of the obligation of justice and charity towards one's neighbor, towards the communities to which one belongs and towards society as a whole. In its deepest reality, suicide represents a rejection of God's absolute sovereignty over life and death…" (#66).

Assisted suicide, which Dr. Jack Kevorkian has made a well-known phenomenon, involves helping another person to complete an act of self-destruction. This, the pope says, is "false mercy." True compassion does not lead us to help one another end our lives but to share another's pain. Assisted suicide and euthanasia are acts of betrayal that violate justice and mutual trust, which are the basis of every authentic interpersonal relationship of life.

Our belief in the Resurrection draws us to resist such solutions to suffering and death. The cry of those who are faced with the "temptation to give up in utter desperation" is not a cry for destruction, but rather "a request for companionship, sympathy and support in the time of trial. It is a plea for help to keep on hoping when all human hopes fail" (#67).

These arguments may sound strange to our ears, which have been conditioned by materialism to believe that pain and deprivation overwhelm the human spirit, and by individualism, which denies the reality of our human relationships. If we believe we are totally autonomous individuals, completely separate from others, then the choice to take our lives, or to ask another to help us end our lives, is entirely personal and private. But if we see ourselves as incomplete without the friendships and love of those around us, if we believe that those relationships constitute us and make us fully human, then the choice to take our own lives is indeed an injustice to those friends who actually "own" a part of us. Asking someone else for help in self-destruction is an insult to their love for us.

The importance of pastoral care for the sick and dying and for their loved ones is obvious. At these moments, our hope and faith are stretched thin, and we are in special need of the solace, encouragement, and prayers of others. Chaplains and priests must take their responsibilities in these areas very seriously, shepherding the dying and their families through the valley of death to a clear vision of God's promise of eternal life.

How Should Catholics Vote?

After outlining these threats to the dignity of life, the pope turns to the responsibilities of citizens and politicians in protecting life. He notes that there should be a "continuity" between moral and civil law, since both are rooted in reason and objective truth, and that public laws can never be solely a matter of achieving the will of the majority (#70–72). But he also notes that civil law is more narrow in scope than morality since its purpose is "to guarantee an ordered social coexistence in true justice, so that all may 'lead a quiet and peaceable life, godly and respectful in every way' (1 Timothy 2:2)" (#71).

Laws that legitimize abortion, suicide, or euthanasia in any way are inherently unjust and are in complete opposition to the right to life proper to every person. Willing participation in the passage or execution of such laws, or participation in the intention of those who do, involves direct cooperation with evil and is never permitted. This means that conscientious citizens may never obey such a law or "take part in a propaganda campaign in favor of such a law, or vote for it" (#73). Similarly, medical personnel must refuse direct participation in such "acts against life" and may have to sacrifice their professional positions if they are compelled to participate.

The pope acknowledges that legislators sometimes find themselves in the very difficult position of knowing that they cannot defeat a law that permits abortion or euthanasia; their only choices may be to leave the permissive law as it is or to vote for a measure that reduces, but does not eliminate, the threat to life. In these cases, "when it is not possible to overturn or completely abrogate a pro-abortion law, an elected official, whose absolute personal opposition to procured abortion was well known, could licitly support proposals aimed at *limiting the harm* done by such a law and at lessening its negative consequences…" (#73). In such a case, the legislator is not cooperating with the evil of such a law, but doing her or his best to limit its evil aspects.

The pope refers here to the principle of toleration, which means that we must sometimes settle for less-than-perfect laws that preserve public order but do not eliminate all sinful acts. He refers to a famous passage in the *Summa Theologica* of Thomas Aquinas, in which Aquinas asked, "Whether it belongs to civil law to repress all vice?"[1] Thomas noted that civil laws do indeed allow some vices, or sins, because "human law is framed for a number of human beings, the majority of whom are not perfect in virtue. Wherefore human laws do not forbid all vices, from which only the virtuous abstain, but only the more grievous vices, from which it is possible for the majority to abstain."

He makes a similar point in reference to the rites of unbelievers, which in the time of Thomas Aquinas were clearly seen as sinful. The law should tolerate the practice of these rites, Thomas said, because to try to repress them might result in war or civil strife. This would undermine the overall purpose of law, which is to preserve public order. In making his argument,

Thomas drew on the earlier experience of Augustine with the legal toleration of prostitution. While Augustine admitted that prostitution flowed from lust and was morally wrong, he argued that we could not eradicate it by law, and that trying to do so would result in a worse situation in which "society was convulsed by lust." Though far from a perfect solution, he said, we should be content to limit prostitution as much as possible and thus preserve public order.[2]

The parallel with abortion is this: even though many people recognize abortion as killing of the innocent, and therefore morally wrong, we may have to tolerate laws that allow some abortions because many members of society do not share our views and would not obey more restrictive laws. Trying to make abortion illegal would not eliminate it and would also result in an industry of illegal abortions—which would undermine the overall purpose of the law. So in some cases the best we may be able to do is to gradually reduce the number of abortions by a number of means, legislative and social, while tolerating them legally, though by no means approving of them, in the meantime. This involves the cultivation of political patience on our part as we realize that moral perfection and political peace are achieved gradually and over a long period.

Voting for the Common Good

When Catholics go to the polls, they should remember first of all that a moral consensus among Christians, Jews, Muslims, and nonbelievers is possible—but that it is an elusive reality and is achieved only with dialogue and patience. As we prepare to vote, we should listen to different moral opinions carefully, sifting them for what is truly human and valid. The goal of our political life is not to impose the superiority of one religious view over another, but to find a kind of compromise that will enable us all to live in peace. This will not make us moral. But it will provide the environment in which we are able to pursue morality and train our children in it. At times, public policy will seem painfully thin or even deficient. But we must remember that it is not an end in itself but only a precondition for the real purpose of our lives.

Our voting should also involve a careful analysis of all the positions a candidate offers. It will be rare that we find one candidate who supports every value we hold, but we should always try to find the best combination. The key here is *the common good*. Which candidate offers the best hope, overall, of providing for all the things we need in common: education, economic stability, protection of life, medical care, public safety, and defense? Selecting a candidate on the basis of his or her views on only one topic is almost always a mistake. No single value, no matter how important, is an adequate guide for the complex task of government, which exists to make our life in common and the pursuit of our individual goals possible.

"You Did It To Me: For a New Culture of Human Life"

Perhaps the most important part of *Evangelium Vitae* is the last section, in which the pope describes how the promotion of a "culture of life" is everyone's responsibility. Although he focuses on the importance of good legislation and the role of faith in preserving human life from the indignity of abortion, suicide, euthanasia, and capital punishment, in this last section he emphasizes that the gospel of life is not for believers alone: "life has a sacred and religious value...that every human being can grasp by the light of reason" (#101). It is the whole of human society that must work for the common good by acknowledging and defending the right to life.

Christians are people who have been sent to preach the gospel of life, and we have a responsibility not just to limit the influence of evil but to "*celebrate* [life with] our whole existence, and to *serve it* with the various programs and structures which support and promote life" (#79). In the final section of *Evangelium Vitae*, Pope John Paul II describes the duties that fall to many different classes of persons in preaching this gospel and promoting the beauty and dignity of human life.

He addresses first teachers, catechists, and theologians, who must illustrate the "anthropological reasons" upon which respect for human life is based. It is their duty to show what human life is and how our choices can protect it. They are also responsible for the formation of conscience and the cultivation of liturgical and private prayer, enriched by the symbols and gestures of our own tradition and those from other cultures and peoples. Such prayer fosters contemplation and draws us into a community that rejoices in the gift of life. Our daily living is part of our spiritual worship when it is filled with praise, gratitude, and generosity. This should include "gestures of sharing" such as organ donation.

We must also encourage vocations to service, and a rededication to serving others that will help promote marriage and responsible procreation. Social-service agencies can help meet the challenges of difficult situations by providing care for those afflicted with drug addiction, mental illness, and AIDS as well as those who struggle with disabilities or the infirmities of old age. Hospitals, clinics, and convalescent homes should be places in which "suffering, pain and death are acknowledged and understood in their human and specifically Christian meaning" (#88). Healthcare personnel and administrators who serve as "guardians and servants of human life" should staff such institutions (#89).

The role of civil leaders is crucial too. They are called to make good choices for the common good, always bearing in mind what is realistically attainable (#90). But the importance of civil leadership should not overshadow the importance of maximum "participation in social and political life" (#93) by all citizens. This is especially important at a time in which political participation is declining because so many citizens have become cynical or apathetic about the role of government. Government need not be seen only as a necessary evil; it can be a means of distributing social goods and organizing human effort in a constructive way. Indeed, in a very enlightening passage that refutes the notion that government is an evil or merely a means of restraining our sinful impulses, Thomas Aquinas affirmed that government would have existed even in paradise. This is so, he said, because humans are naturally social, and even before sin some means would have been necessary to organize life toward the common good.[3] This means that our common life is something for which all of us have a responsibility, not just politicians or government.

Intellectuals have a duty to "offer serious and well documented contributions" promoting life (#98). Those who work in the mass media need "to present noble models of life and make room for instances of people's positive and sometimes heroic love for others" (#98).

He assigns a primary role to the family, or the "domestic church." The responsibility of the family begins with responsible procreation and raising of children.

By word and example, in the daily round of relations and choices, and through concrete actions and signs, parents lead their children to authentic freedom, actualized in the sincere gift of self.…[Their role] also includes teaching and giving their children an example of the true meaning of suffering and death…[and]fostering attitudes of closeness, assistance and sharing towards sick or elderly members of the family" (#92).

Evangelium Vitae states also that the elderly must in some way always remain a part of the family, to reestablish a kind of "covenant" between the generations. While they may be the special object of our concern, our elderly must also be valued for the contribution they make to the gospel of life through "the rich treasury of experiences they have acquired," which make them "sources of wisdom and witnesses of hope and love" (#94).

Pope John Paul II's message calls for a "general mobilization of consciences" to activate a great campaign in support of life (#95). He calls first of all for the renewal of individual hearts, then of the Church itself, the communion of believers, then of political and social life. Such a renewal will help us protect and promote human life wherever it is threatened. He urges us to work in all of these arenas to uncover the brilliant image of God that is planted deep within our lives together, but which has been tarnished by neglect and the narrow pursuit of individual goods.

For Further Reading

Curran, Charles E. "The Difference Between Morality and Public Policy." In *Toward An American Catholic Moral Theology*. (Notre Dame, Ind.: Notre Dame University Press, 1987), 194–203.

Himes, Michael and Kenneth. *Fullness of Faith: The Public Significance of Theology*. Mahwah, N.J.: Paulist Press, 1993.

_____. "The Myth of Self Interest: Hobbes Had It Wrong." *Commonweal* 23 (September 1988): 493–98.

Hollenbach, David. "The Common Good Revisited." *Theological Studies* (March 1989): 70–94.

Chapter 12

Sexual Morality: Wholeness and Holiness

When he wrote his great *Summa Theologica* 750 years ago, Thomas Aquinas made an astonishing statement: "Sex is to the human race what food is to the body." This is a startling assertion because it shows a profound awareness of the centrality of sex to human life—as basic as food itself. Even more important, it suggests that far from being a private act between "consenting adults," as we say today, sex is a highly social reality. Although he does speak of the sexual act as expressive of love and as a sign of marital fidelity, for him the most important thing about sex is that it perpetuates humankind and thus has important social implications.

Why Do People Have Sex?

The fundamental question in sexual morality is "Why do people have sexual intercourse?" The reasons vary, and depending on whether they contribute to human fulfillment or not, they are judged to be either moral or immoral. Most of us would agree that having sex to express love and affection for one's spouse, to start a family, or to renew marital fidelity are good (that is, "moral") reasons to have sex. Using sex as a commodity, as a means to something else (money, prestige, status, security), would be repellent to us; we would see it as literally "selling ourselves." Having sex just for the fun of it, even with people we do not know well, is widely accepted in our culture today, but we would have to agree that such sexual activity falls far short of the kind of intimacy and self-sharing of which sex is capable. And engaging in sex out of vengeance or anger (as in the case of rape) is not only immoral but criminal as well.

Through most of history, one reason for sex—procreation—outweighed all the others. In Thomas's day, for example, the high infant-mortality rate forced women to remain pregnant through the majority of their childbearing years. Some women were pregnant fifteen or twenty times during their lives in order to see six or eight children survive. Procreation was of crucial importance because children were security. In an age when there were no retirement plans or Social Security and the accumulation of wealth was very difficult, a large family was one's only guarantee of economic security. Until recent times it was virtually impossible to live as a single person. One had to have a family—whether a natural one or the adopted family of a monastery or convent—to survive. For the vast majority of the population, there were no real alternatives.

Social conditions in the twentieth century are very different. We are able to put money in the bank, invest in retirement plans, and receive Social Security benefits. Remaining single poses no economic problem. Childlessness, while often regrettable, is no longer the stigma it once was. In fact, couples today can choose to remain childless or to plan their families according to financial or other needs. Since our infant-mortality rate is lower today, and since our economy is structured in such a way that large numbers of offspring are no longer necessary for economic security, people have as many children as they want (often no more than two or three). When they pass the age of childbearing, the purpose of sexual intercourse focuses more directly on expressing love, shaping individual character, bonding as a couple, and "speaking" one's personality or affection. Church teaching has reflected this shift. For centuries, Church documents spoke of the "primary" and "secondary" purposes of sex (procreation and mutual love, respectively). The most recent documents do not distinguish these purposes and see procreation and mutual love as equally important.

While people obviously do have sex to procreate, that is not the only reason they do so. Other reasons for having sex—what theologian Frank

Nichols has called the "surplus value" of intercourse—have taken on a greater importance in our own age.[1] Nichols has said that after the procreative aspect of sex has been realized (which often occurs today by the time people are in their forties, when they have had as many children as they can provide for economically), people still continue to have sex, but for different reasons. At this point, the meaning of sexuality moves away from procreation and begins to focus on other values. Nichols says that at this point in life, sex should be totalizing, so that it involves our whole persons and allows total self-giving; it should be plastic—"not in the sense of artificial, but in the sense of moldable," in such a way that it helps shape us into whole persons; it should also be other-directed, life-giving, and have rich sign value. It should always point beyond itself to the commitment and generativity it signifies.

Sex As Language

These qualities suggest that sex is not just a means to the end of procreation but a language, a way of "speaking ourselves," or a kind of self-communication. Like any other kind of language, sexual language can be spoken well or poorly, tenderly or abusively, honestly or dishonestly, lovingly or manipulatively. Sex can be the violent language of rape, the consumerist language of prostitution, the affirming language of loving marital sex. And like any language, it is learned through imitation and sensory experience. While it continues to develop throughout our lives, the most important years are those of early childhood. As the noted Redemptorist theologian Bernard Häring has said:

> Everyone knows that learning languages, including the child's learning of the mother tongue, necessarily entails the right to make mistakes. Dramatizing a learner's grammatical errors or ridiculing a child's mispronunciations inhibits the learning process. There is something similar in sexual development. The sexual language has to be learned gradually and dramatizing the imperfections and mistakes of childhood leads to the alienation of sexuality.[2]

Scientists today tell us that this sexual language begins forming before birth as hormones shape the brain and sexual organs prenatally. At birth, some of our basic sexual language has already been determined. There is a "maleness" or "femaleness" programmed into our brains before we are even born.

In the early years of childhood, relations with parents, siblings, and others shape the more specific elements of the sexual language—syntax and grammar, if you will. Depending on what these influences are and when they take place, a child's sexual development may be normal and mutual or may become more or less distorted. We know, for example, that a relatively constant percentage of the population is homosexual or bisexual, and that a certain number of others suffer from sexual pathologies that compel them to seek sexual satisfaction with children, or by inappropriate dress or behavior (for example, cross-dressing or stalking), self-inflicted pain, or violence.

In the worst cases, these pathologies become compulsive and criminally destructive. Jeffrey Dahmer and John Wayne Gacy, who were both convicted of mutilating and murdering dozens of young men, are examples of persons whose sexual language was severely deformed. Unable to establish normal, mutual sexual relationships, they could find satisfaction only in sexual activity that was linked to pain and death. These sexual pathologies are virtually impossible to cure because the aberrant desire was impressed deep into the brain at an early age and by a process we do not fully understand. By the time evidence of the desires emerges, it is too late.

Fortunately, such tragic failures in the development of a normal sexual language are rare. But they do remind us that sex is an acquired language, and that parental instruction and example are very important. A good analogy is that of teaching a child to play a musical instrument or learn a foreign language. Children who are taught with love and patience will likely grow up loving the musical or linguistic skill they have acquired. Those whose learning was traumatic, painful, and sprinkled with corporal punishment will probably not only fail to learn to play well, but will hate it besides. Similarly, children who are taught about sex honestly and lovingly, and who see their parents treat each other's bodies and hearts with respect, will be much more likely to learn to speak a sexual language that is whole and life-giving. Children who are taught to associate sex with fear, danger, or punishment will incorporate those features into their sexual language and will be limited in their ability to love and sustain relationships.

Homosexuality presents a special case, in which a child acquires a variant language of sexual self-expression. Scientists are not sure exactly what "causes" homosexuality, but evidence indicates that it is the result of a complex series of prenatal and early-childhood influences. Most specialists agree that sexual identity, homosexual or otherwise, is largely determined by the age of five or six. Homosexuality does not fall into the same category as the sexual pathologies described above because gay men and women can lead happy and productive lives. Although the Catholic tradition says that sexual activity between persons of the same sex lacks the generativity and complementarity necessary for marriage, Church documents stress that all of us—gay or straight—share in the basic dignity God gave us:

> The human person, made in the image and likeness of God, can hardly be adequately described by a reductionist reference to his or her sexual orientation. Everyone living on the face of the earth has personal problems and difficulties, but challenges to growth, strengths, talents and gifts as well.[3]

This suggests that holiness can be found in any state of life. Gay and lesbian persons should strive to find this image of God within themselves, and to realize the values of faithfulness, generativity, self-giving, charity, friendship, and justice as fully as they can. It is important that they are honest about their sexual identity, but they must never reduce themselves to their sexual identity in such a way that they exclude God's grace and love. Similarly, parents of gay or lesbian children must discover and affirm their children's gifts and talents and help them learn how to fulfill the vocation of holiness to which all of us are called.

Sex As Self-Communication

Because sex is not only a means of procreation but a way of intimate self-communication, the Church has always insisted that sex should be reserved to the safety and security of a permanent marital relationship. Just as we hesitate to tell much about ourselves to strangers or to people whom we do not trust, so we should not speak our very selves sexually to someone we do not know or to whom we are not committed. Doing so places us in danger of being hurt by misunderstanding or abuse. Speaking a mature and holy sexual language means knowing when and where to speak it; it means knowing that some things can only be said in protected environments, and that whenever we "speak ourselves" promiscuously or casually, we are hurting ourselves and limiting the great act of self-sharing that sex is.

Sex As a Sacrament

Those of us who were raised in the pre-Vatican II Church remember that a sacrament was defined as "an outward sign instituted by Christ to give grace." We identified those sacraments with the seven specific ritual activities that took place in church or in the confessional. But these specific sacramental moments are rooted in a broader notion of sacramentality that says that God acts through real, tangible things including, but not limited to, bread, wine, water, oil, and the laying on of hands to communicate his presence to us.

This is one of the most distinctive features of Catholic theology. It extends to marriage, in which the couple actually effect the sacrament themselves by speaking their marriage vows (which God then "uses" as an occasion of grace). But it goes beyond the church ceremony and continues into the lives of the married couple whose vows only begin to unfold as the marriage ceremony ends. Their whole lives together become sacramental. Each time they express love, or faithfulness or affection, they create an opportunity for grace to enter into their lives. This grace "builds on" the human acts of love and affection. In an even more profound way, the sexual act itself, as the most intimate experience of married life, becomes the supreme sacrament of marriage. As the couple experiences the pleasure, comfort, and ecstasy of sexual love, they offer God a vast opportunity to enter into their lives. Philip Keane has described this sacramentality:

> Everything about marriage, including its explicitly sexual aspects is part of the sacrament. Past fear of human sexuality may have been part of the reason why the marriage ceremony, rather than the whole marriage, popped into mind when we spoke about "sacrament." But all the married couple's giving to one another and to their children are part of the

sacrament. Sexual intercourse is a major element in the sacramental life of the couple. In this context, it can be understood as a liturgical or worshipful action.[4]

Theologian Denise Lardner Carmody has taken this notion further, linking the holiness of sexuality to the Trinity:

> When we make love, the love of Father, Son and Spirit circulate, come into place....Can it be that the spirit is the kindly light in which we are attractive to one another? Are the excitement, the arousal, the need, the pain we experience relevant to what makes up the life of God?...Human orgasm bespeaks the ecstasy wrought by the divine perfection.[5]

Seen in this way, it is obvious that the fuller the expression of love, the more fully sacramental—that is, revelatory of God—it is. Conversely, when the sexual act is restricted and truncated and conditional (such as when it is between two people who hardly know each other or when it is undertaken only for self-gratification), the sacramental possibility is diminished or even eliminated. The act is too shallow and barren to even bear its own weight much less the weight of God's grace and life.

Sex As Generative

Theologians from Thomas Aquinas down to our own day have spoken eloquently about the essentially procreative nature of sexuality. We have seen how this emphasis was partly due to economic necessity: children were essential to economic survival. But it also bespoke the need for sex to create something outside of itself. In our own age, when lower infant mortality and different economic structures make procreation somewhat less necessary, other reasons, such as the "self-speaking" described above, have emerged as important justifications for sexual intercourse. But even in view of these important developments, one thing remains constant: sex, to be authentic and fully sacramental, must be generative.

Even for couples who cannot or choose not to have children, their marriage and sexual life must continue to generate something outside of itself. The self-speaking and affirmation of the other that takes place in sex is important, of course; but to be like God's own love, which generated all of creation, our love-making must also create and renew. It must first create and renew the partners themselves, enabling them to form a common project that will create and renew those outside of their marriage. In this way, marriage becomes an ongoing sacrament, or sign of God's presence to the world. It is not just a private act between two people, but a powerful witness and social force. Father André Guindon refers to this generative quality as sexual fecundity, which includes, but is not limited to, biological procreation.[6]

The Virtue of Chastity

In an earlier chapter we talked about the virtue of temperance, which has to do with our desires, and which is particularly related to the pleasures of touch. Chastity is a part of the virtue of temperance. Although we sometimes think of chastity as having only to do with restraint, in fact, it is the virtue that helps us integrate our desire for intimacy and sexual pleasure with the rest of our lives. Chastity is not mere abstinence from sex. We may abstain from sex for any number of reasons: fatigue, overwork, fear of punishment, anger. But none of these motives constitutes chastity. The virtue of chastity leads us to forgo sex, not because it is bad, nor because we fear punishment, but because we want to use our sexual ability as it should be used, given our goal in life. We cultivate chastity when we choose sex because it will help us be who we want to be.

Chastity does not eliminate our sexual desire; rather, it trains our desires so that they contribute to a full and satisfying human life. The chaste person is one who is not afraid of or controlled by sexual desire, but who has made desire a normal, healthy part of his or her life. As Ronald Lawler, Joseph Boyle, and William May have written:

> Chastity is the virtue by which a person integrates his or her sexuality into his or her overall Christian vocation.…It can be described as a virtue concerned with the intelligent and loving integration of our sexual desires and affections into our being as persons, enabling us to come into possession of ourselves as sexual beings—and so that we can touch others and allow ourselves to be touched in ways that fully respect the goods of human existence.…Chastity does not seek to suppress or deny sexuality, but rather enables a person to put loving and intelligent order into his

passional life, to take possession of his desires so that the whole self can be at peace.[7]

Vigen Guroian, an Orthodox theologian, has said that marriage (and sex itself) should be an "icon"—not a mere picture of God, but an actual window on the divine.[8] Can we see sex as such a powerful gift? Can we link our explicitly sexual moments with the great wonder of sacramental life offered to us in baptism, the Eucharist, and reconciliation? If we can, we are taking an important step toward discovering the fullness of life God has in store for us.

Chapter 13

Morality, Business, and the Meaning of Work

A recent movie adaptation of David Mamet's play *Glengarry, Glen Ross* portrays business gone bad. It is the story of a branch real estate firm that is trying to bolster its sales. The centerpiece of the film is a lengthy monologue by a handsome, soulless downtown executive played by Alec Baldwin. He comes out to give the agents a pep talk about the importance of building sales, no matter what the cost. He pushes overworked and demoralized salesmen into a crude sales competition and tells them that first prize will be a new Cadillac, second prize will be a set of steak knives, and third prize is "you're fired." As the film unfolds, each of the men descends into a moral and emotional pit as they try to meet their family obligations, keep their jobs, or just "play the game." A staccato fire of four-letter words becomes almost unbearable at points and reflects the desperation and poverty of spirit that characterize their lives. The film portrays work as hopeless, demeaning, and destructive. Far from humanizing them, their work has turned them into competing animals who lose respect for their managers, their clients, and themselves.

Glengarry, Glen Ross is a brilliant work, but it is frightening and vulgar because it paints in bold strokes the effects of inhuman work, which all of us have at least tasted in the drudgery, low pay, tyrannical bosses, impossible working conditions, or lack of job security that can characterize work.

Business ethics has become very popular today as corporations begin to see themselves as moral entities that act with freedom and purpose much as individual persons do. Yet too often, business ethics means nothing more than a "code of conduct," or even a set of "customary practices" that may only articulate what is usually done, rather than what should be done. Even the best codes of ethics too often focus only on what to do. But since work is at once the most basic commodity of business and the most widespread human activity, business ethics should really begin with what it means to work.

Ways of Looking at Work

At one level, work is a commodity that companies purchase and employees sell to finance their own ends. But unlike other commodities, work is also a means of self-realization and self-perfection. A company may buy a hundred pounds of a raw material and "use it," but work involves using human capital toward the perfection of two products: that which will be manufactured and sold, and the worker herself, who will be affected by the work she does, who learns and develops as she works and is able to add more value to the productive enterprise. Work is a way in which we become more fully persons. It has a personal meaning for us, and it also has a theological meaning.

Scripture tells us that God worked, and then rested. It also tells us that after God worked, God shared dominion or authority over creation with human persons, making our work an act of co-creation with God. But Scripture also says that because of sin we are condemned to "work by the sweat of our brows." Depending on which of these views we hold, work takes on a very different meaning.

Work As Punishment for Sin?

Theologian Francis Fiorenza has suggested that we may see work as merely a punishment for sin, as "just a job" that has to be done to survive, but from which we have no right to expect any satisfaction or happiness. This was Henry Ford's original justification for the assembly line.[1] In this view, we put up with our work, but we don't "enjoy it," nor does it make us better persons. If we see our work as "co-creation," however, our labor is linked to the creative work of God and tries to "create something," even if it is only an attitude within. It is the difference between two stonemasons: one is just cutting stone, the other is building a cathedral. If my work is linked to God's creative work, then I am linked to God so that what I do gives me dignity and holiness. My work is no longer just a drudgery that I endure to make a living, but it is a creative act that makes something useful to others, and makes me a better person. I participate in the result, not just the process.

When someone says, "I love my work," that usually means that their work not only fabricates, but creates: it fulfills, enhances, and improves their lives and the lives of others. In this sense, their work is sacramental. Like the bread and wine at Mass, which are "the fruit of the earth and work of human hands," meaningful work is work that makes God's own transforming power present. Frequently, those who experience work "as its own reward" are engaged in the arts or in the healing, teaching, or service professions. But not always. Other jobs, even more mundane and repetitive ones, can also become sacramental if managers are sensitive to the potential of work not only to make products and profit, but to make persons more human.

Thomas Smith has done a fine job of showing how this can happen, even in menial jobs. In his book *God on the Job: Finding God Who Waits at Work,* he has described "workfaith," which combines the reality of work and the reality of faith and relates it to a number of different kinds of work. He takes the example of factory workers who make boxes:

> The first step in clarifying the workfaith dimension of any job is to state the nature of the job in simple and basic terms. What does this work activity do or provide? Box makers, for example, produce containers designed to hold things. Boxes make it possible to move or store quantities of items and protect them from damage.…Box makers are in the protection and transportation business. One workfaith connection for box makers is to reflect on this protection in the light of creation.…The purpose of boxes is to protect other items that can trace their history to God.…[2]

Smith continues with other examples that show how electricians, mechanics, counselors, and secretaries can all find theological and faith meaning in their work.

The Vices of Business

Although the word is seldom used today, a "vice" is an acquired manner or "habit" of doing things. Like people, businesses have certain characteristic ways of acting, certain practices or habits that are virtuous and others that are not. Like every sphere of human life, business has certain characteristic vices. These vices, or tendencies to sin, take a variety of shapes, but they all militate against the sacredness of work. Because work is so essential to what it means for business to be "ethical," let us suggest a few of the most prevalent of these "vices."

What We Make: Socially Responsible Production

The first question responsible businesses must ask themselves is whether their products are truly useful. Stores are full of things that may be amusing or entertaining but are far from the core of human life. Yet they are aggressively marketed as "needs," and people who have discretionary income buy them. More serious is the manufacture and marketing of things that are not only unnecessary but destructive. Certain kinds of handguns and automatic weapons, which have little beneficial use to citizens in a free society, may be one example. Unhealthy foods and unsafe toys or vehicles are others. On a larger scale, excessive military production, especially in an era when superpower competition has disappeared, is unnecessary and possibly even dangerous. While it is true that the military industries provide jobs, corporations are bound to ask themselves how they can turn their productivity to things that are not only productive of work, but of human dignity and fulfillment.

Since industries that produce harmful or dangerous products grew to their present size over a long period, it is not reasonable to expect that they can convert their ingenuity to more beneficial means overnight. But conscientious managers and boards will examine the inherent quality and value of what they manufacture. They will ask, "Does society benefit from this product?"

Quality of Production: How We Make It

In addition to asking, "What do we make and how does it improve life?" managers must also ask, "How do we make it?" This question includes asking about working conditions, compensation, profit sharing, participation in management, and the need for workers to be able to take pride in the quality of what they make. The American auto industry has learned this lesson the hard way: they were outsold by foreign manufacturers whom consumers saw as making a better product at a lower price. U.S. auto manufacturers have begun to recoup their sales by devoting greater attention to quality and workmanship, and by giving workers more control over the manufacturing process. This not only makes the product more appealing but gives workers more pride and job satisfaction as well.

Isolationism

Americans are talking a great deal today about whether we are becoming politically isolationist, that is, turning a blind eye to the economic and political needs of the rest of the world, "minding our own business" but neglecting our moral duty to help those outside our borders who are in need.

Businesses can suffer from a certain kind of isolationism, too, when they act as though they are not really part of society, or as though they are not really responsible for the effects of their business practices. Much current business-management theory focuses on "social responsibility." This is a first step. But corporate attempts at social responsibility can fail if they dress a company up in nice, ethical clothes but fail to really engage the company with the society in which it operates and from which it draws its profit. A company engages the society in which it exists when it not only responds to crises, but asks itself—before a crisis emerges—how it can best contribute to the well-being of that society. It is the difference between paying for the cleanup of chemical spills and taking steps to prevent spills in the first place. Today's corporations are so large and wield so much influence that they do not always have to capitulate to "the way things are." By the way they invest, hire, nurture workers, and contribute to education and healthcare, they can explore and sometimes bring about "the way things ought to be." Engagement acknowledges the implicit contract that emerges when a company is incorporated: society is saying, in effect, "We grant you permission to organize for the sake of doing business, but in return we expect a certain contribution of taxes, positive influence, and constructive cooperation."

The Virtuous Manager

Finding all this meaning in work, especially for employees who have dull, repetitive jobs, is no easy task. It is not unlike the job of a priest who, acting in the person of Christ, takes ordinary elements like bread and wine and makes them sacred, holy "occasions of grace." It demands that managers not only be good accountants but persons of character: holy persons who are so deeply rooted in truthfulness, justice, and vision that they cannot easily be compromised. This enables them to transform their organizations and renew the experience of work.

Two virtues are particularly important to businesspersons. The first is the virtue of prudence, the moral skill of knowing what is to be done. Prudence, as we showed in chapter 7, is the ability to know what the goal is and to know how to go about achieving it. It requires taking general principles and applying them effectively to the matter at hand. Most often in business, the goal equals a profit. Successful managers are those who know how to use human and financial resources to make a product and a profit. They must be able to use past experience well and to see future consequences; they must know when to consult and when to make a decision; they must know when to "go by the book" and when to try something different to achieve a good effect in unusual circumstances. The prudent manager is not just cautious but effective, someone who can "see the whole picture" and make the right move at the right time.

Justice is another important virtue in business. It means creating honest relationships with suppliers, customers, and employees and seeing that each of these groups "receive their due." Justice involves truthfulness and quality, as well as compensation for goods and services proportionate to their real worth. In our modern world, justice in business also means taking no more from the earth than we have a right to. More and more, corporations are seen as holding natural resources in trust for all of us.

Companies that use these resources recklessly for their own benefit are seen as violating the rights of the rest of us who together "own" these resources.

Fortitude, or the courage that enables us to seek a good that is difficult to achieve, is also important. Businesspeople are under great pressure to make a profit. This sometimes causes them to consider doing unjust or unethical things. Fortitude can help them "do the right thing," even when there is an easier way. More humane but less profitable downsizing, fair treatment of competitors, revealing errors in a contract that serve one's own interests are all difficult but noble things requiring fortitude.

Peter Senge has said that corporations must become "learning organizations" that are "committed to the development of all people's ability to create the life they want." It is not just creating a series of individual lives, but a common life, a common good, a society. It is a question of helping to guide employees to see that their work is not just a means to a new boat or a second home or even a college education, but a way of seeing the sacred, and finding the Spirit, even in the act of assembling a table or entering data.

Thomas More, author of *Care of the Soul,* has said that "work is liturgy" and that we can help workers bridge the gap between "the sacred and the secular by occasionally ritualizing the everyday things we do. We might buy tools of satisfying quality, well made, pleasing to look at, fitted to the hand, or an office desk of special design or select woods." Our work should be creative. This does not mean it must be exceptional, but that it should always "make something for the soul." The virtuous manager will help each and every employee nurture the soul, even if only by improving the manner of doing a task that does not have great intrinsic meaning.

Sacramentality in the Workplace

Each business has to explore its own potential for sacramentality and find ways in which employees (and employers) can become better, holier people through their work. Yet there are at least a few general principles that apply to all.

Subsidiarity

The principle of subsidiarity is one of the bedrocks of Catholic social teaching. It says that decisions should always be made at the lowest level of organization. Subsidiarity (in business or government) gives persons as much freedom as possible and removes decision-making authority from them only when it is in the interest of the whole group or enterprise to do so. One way of achieving this aim is broad consultation, but in large corporations this is often not feasible. Today some corporations have gone beyond consulting employees to what is sometimes called "demassification."[3] This theory actually calls for the breaking down of a large corporation into smaller organizational units, sometimes even creating discrete companies within a company, which function independently but within the sphere of the larger organization. The theory is that demassification gives people more ready access to and control over data, production, and working conditions and creates happier workers and a better product. However it is envisioned, any kind of subsidiarity that empowers more people and keeps all decisions from rising to the top will make the workplace more satisfying.

Mission and Ownership

All of us find it difficult to work for an organization we do not understand. If I am responsible only for moving part X from location A to location B, but have no idea what happens to it before or after my action, my participation in the overall mission of the organization is limited, and my potential for frustration is high. If, on the other hand, I know why the organization exists, what its final product looks like, what it takes to make the product, and the external market forces that affect production, my involvement will be much better informed and more enthusiastic. As president of a school, I have found that I can never reiterate or discuss the mission of our institute too much. The more I do, the more all the faculty and staff are able to buy into it and help shape it for the future. If the mission of my organization is my possession alone, it will receive only the very limited nurturance I am able to give it.

Connectedness

In his book *The Great Game of Business,* Jack Stack has noted the importance of setting specific goals for employees, almost creating a game in which the finish line is clear to everyone so that people can work together in reaching it.[4] There is sometimes a temptation on the part of employers to keep the "bottom line" or the "big picture" secret or obscure, for fear that employees will find out too much or become discouraged or meddlesome. Stack's theory is that it is far more helpful to set big goals and break them down into smaller goals for each unit. This helps employees feel connected and makes their work more meaningful by giving them a real stake in the outcome and enables them to see exactly what their efforts contribute to the overall result.

Communication

Nothing is more frustrating to employees than being kept in the dark. When managers fail to keep employees and staff aware of the mission, of reasons for changes, of impending problems, they risk the loss of confidence and cooperation. Sometimes, lack of communication is deliberate. Other times, it is a matter of inertia: the manager says, "I already told them that twice." However, hearing something and hearing it when it is pertinent are not the same. Many memos and talks are forgotten because the information is not given at the right time. Good communication involves not only knowing what needs to be said, but when.

The heart of an ethical business is a virtuous manager. The virtuous manager is one who doesn't just "know the rules" but one who cultivates truthfulness, communication, appreciation for the dignity of each worker, and real engagement with society and respect for the covenant his company has with society. She is also someone who always aims at the common good of the company, society, and even the globe.[5] A far cry from Alec Baldwin's character in *Glengarry, Glen Ross,* virtuous managers are those who keep workers "connected" so that they don't just work for a company but participate in it. A virtuous manager would also learn how to make work sacramental so that it is not experienced as the penalty for sin but as a gift of cocreation with God.

For Further Reading

Williams, Oliver, and John Houck. *A Virtuous Life in Business: Stories of Courage and Integrity in the Corporate World.* Lanham, Maryland: Rowman and Littlefield, 1992.

Notes

Introduction

1. Michael Duffy, *Be Blessed in What You Do: The Unity of Christian Ethics and Spirituality* (Mahwah, N.J.: Paulist, 1988).

Chapter 1: The Changing Shape of Christian Morality

1. William Cosgrove, "How Celtic Penance Gave Us Personal Confession," *Doctrine and Life* 41 (Oct. 1991): 412–22.

2. From the Bigotian Penitential (ninth century), I. Cited in A. Bieler, *The Irish Penitentials* (Dublin: 1963).

Chapter 3: Sources of Moral Wisdom: Experience, Reason, and Scripture

1. See "John A. Ryan" in Charles Curran, *American Catholic Social Ethics* (Notre Dame, Ind.: Notre Dame University Press, 1982), 26–91.

2. Yves Congar, O.P., *Sacramental Worship and Preaching,* Concilium 33 (Mahwah, N.J.: Paulist, 1968), 62.

Chapter 4: Conscience As Our Moral Compass

1. *The Responsible Christian: A Popular Guide for Moral Decision Making According to Classical Tradition* (Chicago: Loyola University Press, 1984).

Chapter 5: Fundamental Choices for Good and Evil

1. William Pfaff, "The Pope Identifies American Problem," *Los Angeles Times* (Oct. 1, 1993).

2. Peter Steinfels, "Beliefs," *New York Times* (Oct. 16, 1993).

Chapter 7: Let Virtue Be Your Guide

1. Servais Pinckaers, O.P., "Virtue Is Not a Habit," *Cross Currents* (Winter 1962): 65–79.

2. Philip Keane, *Christian Ethics and Imagination* (Mahwah, N.J.: Paulist, 1984).

Chapter 8: Liturgy, Friendship, and the Moral Life

1. "Slaying in the Spirit" refers to a faint in which an individual, emotionally overwhelmed by the presence of the Spirit, falls backward, prostrate and motionless. Unfamiliar to most Catholics, this experience is common among Pentecostal Christians. See "Charismatic Pastoral Care" in *Dictionary of Pastoral Care and Counseling,* ed. Hunter (Nashville, 1990). See also Christopher Kiesling, O.P., "The Seven Quiet Gifts of the Holy Spirit," *Living Light* 23 (1986): 137–50. Also John Mahoney, "The Spirit and Moral Discernment in Aquinas" and "The Spirit and Community Discernment in Aquinas" in *Seeking the Spirit: Essays in Moral and Pastoral Theology* (Denville, N.J.: Dimension Books, 1981).

2. Paul Waddell, *The Primacy of Love: An Introduction to the Ethics of Thomas Aquinas* (Mahwah, N.J.: Paulist Press, 1992), especially chapter 4, "Charity: The Virtue of Friendship With God."

Chapter 9: Personal Responsibility for Healthcare

1. Daniel Callahan, "High Tech or Long-Term Care? Let the Elderly Decide," *New York Times* (June 12, 1994): 15.

2. Norman Paradis, "Making a Living Off the Dying," *New York Times* (June 12, 1994).

3. Philip Keane, *Health Care Reform: A Catholic Perspective* (Mahwah, N.J.: Paulist, 1993).

Chapter 11: Morality and Public Life: Political Choices in a Diverse Society

1. Thomas Aquinas, *Summa Theologica,* 1–2, q. 96, a. 2. Cited in *Evangelium Vitae,* #71, note 92.

2. Thomas Aquinas cites Augustine's opinion in this matter in *Summa Theologica* (2-2, q. 10, a. 12): "Thus Augustine says, 'if you do away with harlots the world will be convulsed with lust.' Hence, though unbelievers sin in their rites, they be tolerated, either on account of some good that ensues, or because of some evil avoided (e.g., scandal or disturbance)."

3. "[Political] dominion would have existed in the state of innocence for two reasons: first of all because we are naturally social…and the social life of many is not possible unless someone presides who can direct the group toward the common good.…Second, because if one man greatly surpassed another in knowledge and justice, it would be all wrong if he did not perform this function for the benefit of others…" (*Summa Theologica* I, q. 96, a. 4).

Chapter 12: Sexual Morality: Wholeness and Holiness

1. Frank Nichols, "Sexuality Fully Human," *The Furrow* (March 1983): 145–54.

2. Bernard Häring, *Free and Faithful in Christ: Moral Theology for Clergy and Laity*. 3 vols. (New York: Crossroad, 1981), 2:504.

3. Congregation for the Doctrine of the Faith, "The Pastoral Care of Homosexual Persons" (Oct. 1, 1986): #16.

4. Philip Keane, *Sexual Morality: A Catholic Perspective* (Mahwah, N.J.: Paulist, 1977), 65.

5. "Doing Sexual Ethics in a Post-Permissive Society," *The Way* 28 (1988): 244ff.

6. André Guindon, *The Sexual Creators: An Ethical Proposal for Concerned Christians* (Lanham, Md.: The University Press of America, 1986). See chapter 4, "Toward a Renewed Notion of Sexual Fecundity."

7. Ronald Lawler, Joseph Boyle, and William May, *Catholic Sexual Ethics* (Huntington, Ind.: Our Sunday Visitor, 1985), 127–32.

8. Vigen Guroian, *Incarnate Love: Essays in Orthodox Ethics* (Notre Dame, Ind.: University of Notre Dame Press, 1987). See especially chapter 4, "An Ethic of Marriage and Family."

Chapter 13: Morality, Business, and the Meaning of Work

1. Francis Fiorenza, "Religious Beliefs and Praxis: Reflections on Catholic Theological Views of Work," *Work and Religion* (Concilium #131), ed. Gregory Baum (New York: Seabury, 1981), 92–117.

2. Thomas Smith, *God on the Job: Finding God Who Waits at Work* (Mahwah, N.J.: Paulist Press, 1995), 59–60.

3. See Mitch Finley, "Smaller is Beautiful," *Business Ethics* (January/February 1993): 30ff.

4. Jack Stack, *The Great Game of Business* (New York: Doubleday, 1990).

5. See Raymond Baumhart, "It's Not Easy Being a Manager and a Christian," *America* (May 4, 1991): 486–89. He discusses the manager's responsibility for the common good on page 487.

Index

About the Author

Charles E. Bouchard, O.P., is a Dominican priest ordained in 1979. He received his doctorate in moral theology from the Catholic University of America in 1987 and currently serves as president and assistant professor of moral theology at Aquinas Institute of Theology in St. Louis, Missouri. He teaches, writes, and lectures in the area of fundamental morality, sexual ethics, and healthcare ethics. He has written numerous articles on moral issues for the *Liguorian* and writes a regular column on business ethics for the *St. Louis Business Journal.* Other publications include "Authentic Preaching on Moral Issues" in *In the Company of Preachers* (Collegeville, Minn.: Liturgical Press, 1992); "Morality and the Problem of Sexual Addiction" (*The Priest,* 1986); "The N.R.A. and Gun Control" (*Chicago Studies,* August 1989); "Sexual Identity and Religious Identity: Closing the Gap" (*Review for Religious,* 1990); and "Making Moral Decisions: A Practical Guide" (*Church,* 1991).